Breakthrough to Higher Psychism

TORKOM SARAYDARIAN

T.S.G. PUBLISHING FOUNDATION

Visions for the Twenty-First Century®

ISBN: PAPER—0-929874-15-3

Library of Congress Catalog Number 90-90140

Cover Design by:　　*Fine Point Graphics*
　　　　　　　　　　Sedona, Arizona

Printed in the United States of America

Printed by:　　　　*Griffin Printing & Lithograph*
　　　　　　　　　　Glendale, California

Published by:

　　　　　　T.S.G. Publishing Foundation, Inc.
　　　　　　Visions for the 21st Century®
　　　　　　P.O. Box 7068
　　　　　　Cave Creek, AZ 85331-7068 U.S.A.

NOTE: The meditations and prayers contained in this book are given as guidelines. They should be used with discretion and after receiving professional advice.

Table of Contents

Psychic Senses

Psyche means human soul. Each of us is a psyche, a human soul, and the powers of the soul are our own powers.

The soul, the human soul, is located on various levels in our constitution. The higher the level or plane the soul is on, the more evolved he is and the more psychic powers he has.

If you are focused only in your physical body, you have physical powers which are your senses.

Your five senses are psychic powers, powers of the soul. The Spark builds these senses over millions of years during each racial period in which you incarnated many, many times. In the first Race your hearing was developed. In the second Race your touch was developed. In the third Race your sight was built; in the fourth, taste; in the fifth, smell.[1]

Just as you have senses on the physical plane, you also have senses in the emotional body, in the mental body, and in higher bodies.

Real psychic senses are emotional and mental senses, and higher psychic senses are the senses of still higher bodies.

Our physical senses are not yet used to serve humanity. A very small amount of people use their senses to do this. Most people use their senses for their own

---

1. More information is available regarding the Root Races in *Cosmos in Man*, by Torkom Saraydarian (Agoura, CA: Aquarian Educational Group, 1973), pp. 31-42.

survival and pleasure. A day will come in which people will use their senses for the service of all people.

We must take the time to think how our senses can be used for others as tools of service.

Every time our consciousness is focused on a higher plane, the senses and centers of that plane come into action, evolve, and bloom—provided that they are used properly.

There are five avenues of service. Service is

1. Cultivating the potentials of the human soul

2. Helping people to meet their Real Self and the Self of the Universe

3. Helping people to use their existence as a service for humanity

4. Assisting people to bring into manifestation the divinity latent within them

5. Assisting people to learn how to solve their problems

If we want to increase our service, we must refine our senses more and more. To refine means to

— Open new layers of our higher and lower senses

— Raise our focus of consciousness to higher planes or levels

— Give a scientific, realistic approach to our expressions and relationships and thereby avoid vanity, ego, and self-deception

— Establish contacts with higher sources of life

— Express our knowledge, wisdom, and will-power in more creative and more goal-fitting ways

It is interesting to know that our vision is not one hundred percent active. People do not know that they can improve their sight, their vision. The eyes of a simple man and the eyes of an artist are not at the same degree of evolution. This is true for all our senses.

Senses evolve. Our hearing can evolve, our smell can evolve, but unfortunately we have no courses in universities on how to evolve and refine our senses.

Also, we can improve our subtle senses, the senses in the astral and mental planes. Senses evolve and refine in proportion to our expanding consciousness and psychic purity.

To refine means to make our psychic powers operate in their higher gears or in their higher potentials on every plane of our constitution.

Refinement requires that everyday we gradually transcend ourselves, making our senses improve and work at their highest capacity.

The psyche within us has three major powers—

- Intelligence

- Love

- Willpower

—which are manifested through our psychic senses. Intellect leads to omniscience. Love leads to omnipresence. Willpower leads to omnipotence. These three aspects of the soul culminate in the Self and in the All-Self.

Intellect is related to mental development—reason, logic, science, creativity, **knowingness**, unity with the Mind of Cosmos.

Love leads to right relations, cooperation, inclusiveness, understanding, **havingness.**

Will is related to synthesis, to the purpose of life, to the Cosmic Magnet, to **beingness**.

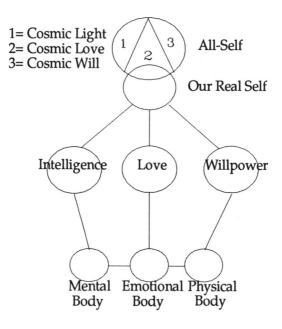

1= Cosmic Light
2= Cosmic Love
3= Cosmic Will
All-Self
Our Real Self
Intelligence   Love   Willpower
Mental Body   Emotional Body   Physical Body

―― **The All-Self and Its projection** ――

Intellect is used to formulate higher inspirations, impressions, and abstract ideas and make them available for humanity. Without a developed intellect, we will stay suspended in abstract dreams.

Love is used to heal, to unite, to encourage, to sacrifice, to sublimate, and to transform. Without your love nature, whatever you know, you have, and you are—all are used against your eternal interest.

By every means try to develop your intellect, your love, and then your willpower.

Try to see how very limited your intellect is and how often it fails to solve your problems but instead leads you into further problems. Once you realize this, you understand why it is so important to cultivate your intellect.

Your love nature also must be developed. No psychic power can be used in the right way unless it is used in love, by love. Try to see how much real love you have for every living being and how you use that love.

Love creates the atmosphere in which the "flowers" bloom. Nothing unfolds its beauty except in an atmosphere of love. The absence of love creates criminals. The more you love others, the more you develop psychic powers.

Willpower makes you master your physical, emotional, and mental nature. When willpower increases in you, you will no longer be the victim of your blind urges and drives. You will never be the victim of glamors, hatred, fear, anger, slander, jealousy, revenge. You will never be the victim of separatism, greed, vanity, ego, illusion.

You cannot make a man master his mechanisms and the various problems of his mechanisms by preaching or advising but only by helping him to develop his willpower.

Willpower is like a sun which disperses the clouds of hindrances from your nature and leads you to live a sacrificial life.

To sacrifice means to do everything possible to bring cooperation, peace, and unity on earth and to reveal the divinity latent in human beings.

The purer is our nature, the clearer will be our reception and translation of impressions coming from higher sources. A person whose physical, emotional, and mental bodies are full of hindrances and impurities will change the nature of an impression and even misuse it, hurting himself and others.

Willpower also creates a shield around us which protects us from psychic attacks or from the attacks of dark forces or dark angels.

Many physical, emotional, and mental sicknesses are the result of contacting higher energies but not being ready for them. Unreadiness means your mechanisms are not able to record and translate properly the incoming inspirations and impressions and are therefore mistranslating them. **This is a major cause of the illnesses of psychics.**

Another cause of illnesses for psychics is astral corpses. Some mediums contact such corpses. When an astral entity dies in the astral plane, he leaves his astral body in the astral world, and this corpse is slowly attracted to the physical plane, especially through mediums. This astral corpse contains all its impressions while it was on earth. These impressions are like tapes which play back through the mental recorder of the medium. The medium thinks that it is an entity that is talking to him or impressing him, but it is nothing but an astral corpse.

The computer of the medium's mind automatically puts these tapes in playback position through associating certain of his own thought-currents to these tapes.

Such a corpse does not stay too long and decays in the astral body of the medium, contaminating him with various sicknesses. Also, it smells very bad, and the medium cannot understand how that malodor emanates from his own body.

Astral corpses also are carried by the dark forces to the rooms of those who do not have a clean life, and there they gradually decompose.

Mediums must be very careful not to hook such a corpse because the price they pay is very high.

To repeat, in order to use our senses for the highest service, they must operate in the increasing light of our intelligence, love, and willpower.

Senses can operate by themselves, or they can be used by other forces. For example, our senses can operate automatically, responding to the stimuli coming from the outer or inner world. They can operate by the force of accumulated impressions within them. They can be operated by certain entities—etheric, astral, and mental—or they can even be operated by evil entities or forces.

One of our duties is to make our senses belong to us and not let them be used by outer stimuli or entities. If our senses are under the control of "strangers," then how can we refine them and use them for the service of humanity?

To serve humanity we should engage ourselves in three kinds of labor.

1. We must develop our psychic powers through expanding our consciousness.

2. We must purify our threefold nature.

3. We must dedicate ourselves to the service of humanity.

Long before other psychic powers are available and safe for us, we must cultivate our intelligence, our pure love, and our willpower. Once these three are developed, we are ready to use higher senses and centers in our emotional, mental, and Intuitional bodies.

The emotional senses are given in the Ageless Wisdom as

a.   astral clairaudience

b.   astral psychometry

c.   astral clairvoyance

d.   astral imagination

e.   emotional idealism

The mental senses are

a.   higher clairaudience

b.   planetary psychometry

c.   higher clairvoyance

d.   discrimination

e.   spiritual discernment

f.   response to group vibration

g.   spiritual telepathy

The Intuitional senses are

a.   comprehension

b.   healing

   c.   vision

   d.   intuition

   e.   idealism

All these senses develop naturally, without any artificial efforts, if a person continuously develops and offers for the service of humanity his intelligence, his love, and his willpower.[2]

The so called lower psychic powers are abnormal growths, and they neither help the owner nor others, except in the short term, while building a heavy karma for the one who uses them for self-interest or to hurt others.

A human being is a personality, later a soul, and eventually the Self.

The personality is the human soul identified with the three bodies simultaneously to make them function as a whole.

The **human soul** is the personality graduated from the three bodies—detached, separated, and in control.

The **Self** is the blooming of the human soul, which gradually releases greater light, love, and power through the three bodies.

As our mental and Intuitional powers or senses unfold together with our intelligence, love, and willpower, we begin to contact

   1. Our Solar Angel

   2. Our Master

   3. Angels

---

2. More information on the senses can be found in *Challenge For Discipleship*, ch. 49 (Sedona, AZ: Aquarian Educational Group, 1986); and *The Psyche and Psychism*, chs. 13, 14, 21, 23, 24 (Agoura, CA: Aquarian Educational Group, 1981), both by Torkom Saraydarian.

4. Higher Beings who function in higher mental and Intuitional Planes

5. Hierarchy

6. Shamballa

Such contacts multiply our usefulness on earth, and we become able to meet the needs of humanity on various planes and guide humanity into right directions, directions that are in harmony with the Plan and the Purpose of life.

In unfolding our psychic powers, we gradually become free. We are no longer trapped by entities who are blind and unintelligent in the etheric, astral, and lower mental planes and who often obsess and possess people, making them believe that they are higher psychics. The truth is that such mediums not only damage themselves but also mislead others and build a heavy karma for themselves in future lives.

Psychics must be highly educated and intelligent persons; they must even have advanced degrees from universities. They must study and expand their consciousness through steady and continuous meditation.

Every psychic must develop his love nature. Unless he is an embodiment of love, higher psychic powers like those which Christ had cannot unfold in him. Christ is in every one of us because He loves us.

The smallest lack of love, the smallest sign of the lack of love, is like a hole in your vessel while sailing the oceans. In the open seas your vessel will sink because of accumulated actions taken without love or against love.

Every psychic must develop his willpower by exercising detachment, striving, renunciation, endurance, patience, serenity, sacrificial labor, perseverance, joy, faithfulness, and dedication. Such efforts increase willpower, which can then be used for the service of humanity.

Every psychic must be tested for his willpower before he is allowed to work with people. A psychic who has no control over his powers will be defeated by these very same powers.

Matter and all forms are eventually conquered by intelligence.

Time is conquered by love.

Space is conquered by willpower, by beingness.

Those who conquer matter can help people conquer their own nature.

Those who conquer time can help people live for the future.

Those who conquer space can help people contact their pure Self.

What happens when you have certain psychic powers, but do not have control over them nor upon your bodies? The answer is that different entities use your mechansims instead of you. Every power that is not under your control can be used by other forces, entities, even beings antagonistic to you. Such entities will mislead you and delay your evolution by leading you from place to place, and by engaging you in different labors that contradict your basic plan and vision in life.

You remember how Christ ordered the winds and waves of the sea to calm down—and they did. This was evidence that His willpower was cultivated to such a degree that it was totally under His control. He did not use entities to do things. He had thousands of Angels around Him but did not use them. He did everything with the power of His Father—the presence of the Most High within Him.

What all psychics must strive for is not to depend on entities and spirits but to depend on the divinity that is within them.

Every psychic eventually is going to be one with the Father within because it is that Presence that contains the most precious psychic powers, ready to be used for the service of humanity.

If you are one with a "spirit" but you do not really know who or what it is, you become a "spirit," not a human being. Psychics, if they are not one with the Father within, crack and fall into pieces when their entities or spirits leave them or when they fall into serious problems and crises in the world.

A true psychic is always tested in the **fire of life.**

Some people are proud of their astral or etheric powers of clairvoyance and clairaudience, but they do not know that these powers are inherited from the animal kingdom. Most animals are astrally clairaudient and clairvoyant. This does not make them superior to man. Some clairaudient and clairvoyant people think they are superior to their fellow beings!

Astral clairaudience and clairvoyance in animals are important powers for them. In human beings astral or etheric clairvoyance and clairaudience are hindrances and problem producing factors because these interfere with the intellect and prevent it from growing and unfolding. In addition, human lower psychic powers are used by astral entities to bring more confusion into people's lives.

This is why great Teachers advise us not to be captivated by our lower psychic powers but to devote ourselves to cultivating our intellect, then our Intuition, steadily trying to expand our consciousness with scientific education, meditation, and service. Service especially makes us realize how limited we are and how much knowledge and intellect we need to enable us to serve humanity.

When we begin to cultivate our mind, we see that lower psychic powers slowly disappear, but other higher powers come onto the horizon of our being. These are the mental and Intuitional senses and powers which, as we eventually unfold, lead us toward superhuman evolution.

To sum up, to be higher psychics we need to cultivate our intelligence to the highest degree we can. We must cultivate our love-wisdom and develop our will-power to gain mastery over our lower self. Then we will use all our talents, our thoughts, our feelings, our words, our actions for the service of humanity.

How can we refine our psychic powers and offer them for the service of humanity?

We can do this by refining our bodies and our consciousness, by trying to manifest our inner divinity, by feeling responsibility toward whatever is going on in the world, and by trying to meet the needs of the world.

The Hierarchy is the greatest source of guidance because every one of Them has graduated with a specialized labor. Their focus of awareness is on the Buddhic, Atmic, and Monadic Planes, so They have a wide, overall view of what is going on.[3] Also, They are the inhabitants of the two worlds—subjective and objective—whereas the **spirits**, or astral or mental enti-

---

3. More information on the higher planes can be found in the *Science of Becoming Oneself*, ch. 14, by Torkom Saraydarian (Agoura, CA: Aquarian Educational Group, 1982).

ties, are not grounded people. They see things mostly from the viewpoint of the plane in which they live. It is not wise to take their opinions and directions because their information and knowledge is limited. Besides, their motives are not always right.

Approach to the Hierarchy is through your Solar or Guardian Angel because this Angel is a member of Hierarchy and works in cooperation with Hierarchy. Your Solar Angel is the door by which to enter into the subjective kingdom and to come in contact with the denizens of the subjective world.

When Christ said that those who do not enter through the door are thieves, He was not joking. If you want to enter into the higher planes, even to come in contact with the members of Hierarchy, it must be through your Solar Angel. So you must develop a communication line between you and your Solar Angel. This line is built through three steps.

1. Through cultivating virtues such as

— solemnity

— purity

— trustworthiness

— nobility

— sense of responsibility

— compassion

— gratitude

— patience

— perseverance

— enthusiasm

— faithfulness

— righteousness

2. Through the following activities

— meditation

— study of the Ageless Wisdom

— sacrificial service

3. Through obeying the slightest suggestions of your heart or conscience and living in the Inner Presence.

The signs of contact with your Solar Angel are as follows:

— psychic energy

— purity of motive

— joy

— freedom

— creativity

— service

— trustworthiness

How does your Solar Angel guide you?

1. Through sudden thoughts, flashes of Intuition

2. Through dreams

3. Through symbolic visions

4. Through direct musical notes with special qualities

5. Through fragrance

6. Through verbal instructions

7. Through touches

8. Through creating tendencies

9. Through magnetic currents

— 2 —

One Consciousness

The human etheric body is a network of communication between the subtle or energy part of the Universe and the etheric centers. The etheric centers use the etheric body to communicate with the etheric body of any object, even of remote planets.

As our etheric centers increase their multi-dimensional activities and awaken one by one, they will have greater and more accurate contact with the Universe. Remember that any object contacted with all our five physical senses is understood better than if we made contact with only one sense.

The seven centers in the etheric body are like the seven senses of the etheric body. They develop slowly, gradually, as we create the right conditions for their development.

Some people have their etheric centers or chakras developed to a certain degree. We can refer to these people as psychics or higher psychics.

When a person develops his centers and senses to a higher degree, all the Universe stands for him as an open book. This is the Book of Life. A higher psychic can read any part of this book, as if it were a hologram. For higher psychics, time and space slowly disappear because they themselves are the observers in all phenomena.

This is a hologram:

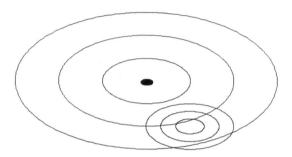

In observing the small hologram, you see the entire image of existence.

In this hologram you have a whole and a portion and an observer. But in a more advanced stage you are not an observer; you are the object and you are the observing object. You are aware of all your All-ness.

True knowledge is in beingness, not in knowingness, nor is it even derived through communication. One cannot communicate with himself. He does not need to communicate if he is himself. He does not need to communicate with the Universe. He is the Universe.

The process of becoming the Universal Whole is achieved through naturally unfolding the seven chakras of the etheric body and the senses of the astral, mental, and Intuitional Planes.

Very high level identification with the Universe is achieved when the Intuitional Plane begins to operate.

Our Solar System has four Cosmic frequencies which contain the image of all that exists in our Solar System.

The lowest Cosmic Ether is the Intuitional Plane, also called the Fourth Cosmic Ether. Then we have the Third, the Second, and the First, the highest Cosmic Etheric Plane, which is sometimes called the Divine Plane.

These Cosmic Ethers are used through a network of communication lines, called the Antahkarana, which is directly related to the senses and chakras of all planes. When they are in communication, the following occur:

a. We are aware of all that is going on in our Universe.

b. Then we are in all that exists in the Universe.

c. Then we are all that Is.

For psychologists and scientists, there are various kinds and levels of consciousness. This is true as long as you are on the path of studying the subject of consciousness, but in reality there is only One Consciousness, and every other consciousness is limited, or an imprisoned drop of consciousness, subject to providing the needs of the person.

The Consciousness, in reality, is One. The more you renounce the differentiation of your consciousness, the more you become a conscious part of that One Consciousness. This is the goal of all living beings: to be one with that All-Consciousness. It is the All-Con-sciousness that transcends time and space because It is Beingness.

When one's consciousness is unified with the All-Consciousness, he is

— omniscient

— omnipresent

— omnipotent

Those who are working toward this purpose need learning, knowledge, bridges, roofs, and vehicles. Then eventually all these will be discarded, once you reach "Home" and become part of the All-Consciousness.

In the All-Consciousness level, all manifestation is the same and has the same image, "The Image of God." It is not necessary to search, to learn, to know. The knower, the knowledge, and the object of knowledge are One.

An emancipated consciousness sees the uniformity in everything. A consciousness that is identified with the All-Consciousness sees himself in everything, in every object. The All-Consciousness watches all that is going on in every life-form as an observer and witness. The more your consciousness expands, the more aware you become of the life in the vast Universe.

3

The Self

The Self is the treasury within us. Our Core, which contains in Itself the entire splendor of the Universe, must come into manifestation.

Our greatest glory and honor is built in the process of actualizing our True Self. We are going to manifest the beauty which is hidden in each one of us. The percentage of our manifestation of beauty is equal to what we are, factually.

The next aspect of Self is goodness. The more goodness we manifest in our life, the more Self we are. **Goodness is like the Sun which radiates to every form without expectation.**

A disciple is one who takes a bulldozer and runs over the buildings that he has constructed during millions of incarnations. He gradually wipes them out to prepare the foundation for a glorious future. This is what Self-actualization is.

You must not construct a hundred story building without a proper foundation. A foundation is your pure Self, devoid of all the trash that you have accumulated around it. The foundation is also called sincerity, simplicity, and purity. Without these factors it is impossible to have a foundation. Sincerity, simplicity, and purity are characteristics of the True Self.

Try to radiate goodness through your thoughts, expressions, words, motives, and actions, and you will feel how real you are. Slander, envy, gossip, and treason keep you a slave in an illusionary world because they destroy the formation of your soul.

The Self is all loving, all understanding, all giving, and the more Self you are, the less people dare to manipulate your goodness.

The Self's only interest is to bloom and flower toward the Cosmic Self.

People must be good to their bodies and heart and mind. If you are doping your body, doing things against your conscience, or acting against the welfare and freedom of others, you are not good to yourself. If you are building a heavy karma for yourself by exploiting others, you are not good to yourself.

Doing goodness to yourself and others is a process of Self-actualization. In the advanced path you not only live a life of goodness, but you yourself also become an embodiment of goodness. Such was the Lord Buddha.

Some modern psychologists understand "Self-actualization" in a different way. They tell us to express our anger in violent ways, to express sex in various ways, to express our hatred and jealousy in still other various ways. These people have no idea about the Self. The Self for them is anger, hate, sex, jealousy, revenge. These are acts of Self-defeat. Trying to express your anger, sex, hate, revenge, etc., in order to get rid of them, is like trying to eliminate a cup of poison by dumping it down your throat.

The Self is beyond such vices. It is Beauty, Goodness, and Righteousness. Righteousness must be expressed throughout our life in our thoughts, words, and actions. The more righteous we are, the closer we are to our Core. How righteous we are toward our body, heart, brain, wife, husband, children, neighbors, authorities, teachers, is how much righteousness we practice. Righteousness brings out the beauty and goodness that we are in our essence.

There was a mechanic who, one day, changed the oil in my car and in the meantime was talking about how righteous he was in all his relationships. After the oil was drained in a pan, he took it and dumped it under a huge tree. I moved close to him and said, "What a righteous fellow you are!"

The mechanic asked, "What is the matter?"

I asked, "How can you pour that poison on the roots of that magnificent tree?"

"Well, I must dump it somewhere," he said.

We must accept and cherish the rights not only of people but also the rights of animals, trees, and the soil. To respect and understand the rights of life-forms means to be righteous.

We must face ourselves often and check if we are trying to be really beautiful, to have goodness in our heart and righteousness in all our relationships. This leads us to Self-actualization. Every time we act ugly, with evil intention, or become unrighteous, we accumulate hindrances on our path and make it difficult to reach our future destination.

If we imagine having had five hundred incarnations and doing ten ugly things in each life, can you imagine how many obstacles we have accumulated on our path?

People say, "I am doing many things to shine out my light," but they cannot radiate light because they have built a cement wall around themselves for so many incarnations through ugliness, unrighteousness, and evil intentions.

Karma is the accumulation of those actions which make it very difficult for you to actualize your Divine Self. Every time you prevent your beauty, goodness, and righteousness from being active, you create karma.

Karma means hindrances, obstacles, walls around you. All these one day must be wiped away by your free will or by the force of karma. You will experience much pain to destroy these walls. The more you wait to destroy your obstacles, the more suffering and pain you will pass through.

The best policy in life is not to accumulate karma. The Lemurian and Atlantean civilizations did not see the consequences of the Law of Karma, and they faced a great disaster. Can our Aryan civilization escape from such a destiny?

If we are beautiful, righteous, full of goodness, then the Self will rejoice, and the joy of the Self is the most healing power for our three vehicles.

Our Inner Divinity is trying by all possible means to have a birth, to come into existence. To be in existence does not mean to have a body, feelings, and thoughts; to be in existence means to be Self-actualized, to make our divinity manifest in our life.

People do not realize that most of the time they do not exist. Their body exists, but if you search for their True Self, you meet imitations of It in their emotions and thoughts. The True Self is absent.

To be absent means to have no existence. Most of the people on earth live like vacant houses.

Once I said to a man, "Where are you?"

"I am sitting here."

"That is your body," I said. "It is your body that is sitting there, your emotions are sitting there, your thoughts are sitting there, but someone else is sitting in your body. Where are *you*? You are imitating someone. Someone is acting through you. An imitated image is sitting in you. Where are you, the Self, the Eternal Witness? Is it the Eternal Witness that exists in you, or is it your mechanism that is running by itself?—and you are calling such a mechanical life, 'This is the way I live!' Where is that I?"

People like to imitate movie stars. For example, when an actress changes her hair style, the next day two million girls try to imitate her. If you ask, "What are you doing?" they will say, "I like this kind of hairdo." Do they like it or are they victims of imitation? You run away from your "home" and make your image of imitation live there instead of you. If you find out why you are imitating, you will be closer to Self-actualization.

We are going to come into existence; that is what evolution is. Evolution is the process of coming into existence as divine beauty. Unless we fulfill the purpose of our life and come into existence as the Self, we will become the failures of nature.

In reality, Christ was the manifestation of God. God was successful at coming into manifestation through Christ. The whole mission of Christ was to teach us this fact and to urge us to manifest divinity on earth, to bring God into existence in our lives.

Every time we work against our Self-actualization, we are planning to destroy ourselves. That is how Nature works.

We spoke about Beauty, Goodness, Righteousness, and now we must speak about Joy. Joy is one of the rays of the True Self.

Trying to be joyful is one of the best methods of Self-actualization. Whoever brings joy to the world is the greatest benefactor of humanity because joy is the radiance of God's presence. Whoever is destroying the joy of people is the enemy of his Self. The more joy you bring to yourself and others, the more communication you will have with the Most High, in you and in the Universe.

The actualization of joy is not so easy. You fill yourself with joy. Then a small bug comes and takes away all your joy. But if one wants to actualize his True Self, he will never give up until joy continuously flows down from the mountain of his Self, bringing life and glory to all his thoughts, words, actions, and relationships.

Sometimes your joy evaporates when people gossip about you and slander you, when people borrow money from you and forget to pay it back, or do not feel grateful toward you. If you lose your reputation and prestige, you feel miserable. But if real joy is in the process of actualization, you will not lose your head in storms, and you will never let your songs freeze upon your lips.

There is the joy of achievement, service, devotion, and purity. There is the joy of sacrificing yourself for a great cause. There is the joy of vision and revelation. There is the joy of the awareness of immortality. There is the joy of the awareness that people have forgotten you or did not recognize your service with gratitude. There is the joy of being forgotten. There is the joy of contact and communication with Higher Worlds. There is the joy of paying debts for others. There is the joy of expansion of consciousness, the joy of contacting your Core. All these are phases of Self-actualization.

Joy is the oil of your physical, emotional, and mental mechanisms. Without joy, they burn out and perish. Strangely enough, people sometimes feel happy when they deprive others of joy.

Can you try not to let anyone, anything take your joy away? Can you live in a way that you do not destroy the joys of others? This is a way of kindling the divinity in others.

People lose their joy when they lose their teeth, when their hair becomes white, or when their face wrinkles in old age. Can you keep your joy intact? We have died many times and will die again and again until we come into our true existence, until we actualize our True Self. As long as we do not exist as a Self, we will continuously die and be born. Once we really exist, death will be conquered and we will be immortal.

Unfortunately, we are very often absent. We talk with each other, but we are not there; we shake hands, but we are not there; we eat our breakfast and dinner, but we are not there; we are in the news, in the papers, in our failures, defeats, hatreds, jealousies; yet we are not there.

Who is shaking the hand? Who is talking with that friend? Who is eating that dinner, if you are not there? Very probably you are obsessed and possessed, and you are absent. Try to exist. Try to be present. Try to be there in your actions, talks, and thoughts.

Try to eat your food and do not let an entity in your body eat it, or an anxiety or a hatred eat it. Your food becomes poison when you do not eat it but let "others" in you eat it.

You hug your wife but you are not there. Your wife says, "Honey, you are not real." You say, "I love you," but she says, "Where are you?" If you do not exist, you are a machine. The machine cries, the machine loves, the machine hates, the machine makes love, and the machine eats and watches the news.

Unless you exist, you cannot enjoy life. Joy makes you real, and whatever you do with joy, that deed affects people's lives because you are in your deed. If you are not real, everything in the world has no real value for you, and you misuse everything, manipulate everything, accumulate everything, just to feel that you exist.

Remember the five aspects of the Self: Beauty, Goodness, Righteousness, Joy, and Freedom.

The fifth aspect of the Self is freedom: *Unless you are free, you do not exist.*

How free are you from your body; how free are you from your emotions and thoughts? How much freedom do you have from your vanity and ego and self-interest? The less freedom you have, the less existence you have. Slaves do not exist for themselves but for others. Except you belong to your Self, you do not have a Self.

Freedom is the royal road to Self-actualization because it makes you detach and conquer all those elements in your nature that are not you.

Great Entities in Space, or Great Lives or Beings, are great in comparison to humans, but in comparison to Cosmic Entities, They are like little sparks. Imagine how big we are in the eyes of an ant. We are also like ants in comparison to Great Beings in Shamballa. Some Galaxies are students of other Galaxies. That is how life goes. Thus no one must stop on the Path— satisfied. Each great achievement is the beginning of another one, and another one.

Your Solar Angel often advises you through your friends because sometimes your brain is out of order and cannot be impressed. This is why some of your friends, a father, a mother, dream about you and warn you if necessary.

You must have a diary and record in it any experiences that you have with your Solar Angel: unexpected hints, visions, dreams, voices, or subtle urges and drives, strivings, aspirations, sudden revelations. All these can come naturally from your Solar Angel, but people think they are coming from strange spirits.

You do not even need the guidance of spirits if you have contact with your Solar Angel. Sometimes the contact lasts only a second. You must be alert to catch it.

The Solar Angel communicates with you by giving you clear and important ideas when they are least expected. If you catch them and record them, your contact increases and your Solar Angel develops trust in your readiness.

Your Solar Angel never forces Its will but tries to evoke from you a sensitive response. The Solar Angel is a source of light, love, beauty, and power. The closer you approach It, the more you profit from Its presence.

The Solar Angel tries to create a sensitive response from you through meditation. It is through meditation that It builds a mental communication line between Itself and you. It also communicates through symbols, which It projects toward your mind. Some of your dreams are symbolic conversations, and in thinking about these symbols you develop Intuition.

But through all Its activities, the Solar Angel tries to make us stand on our feet so that we consciously take our evolution into our own hands.

The Solar Angel uses the technique of making you decide to choose to fight for your own survival and provide for your needs, but all these things It does as an invisible presence.

Most of our striving and sacrificial labors are due to Its presence. Its presence inspires us, and we fuse with Its aspirations. Every one of us must have the feeling of worthiness, self-merit, a conviction that we have value. Such a feeling comes by trying to do our best without depending on the Solar Angel. But the Solar Angel is there as a light, as a model of beauty, and as a shield of protection.

The human soul begins to enter into the Spiritual Triad the moment he learns how to sacrifice his time, his possessions, and himself for others. We are told that the path leading from the higher mind to the Intuitional Plane is built by sacrificial service. The more you become sacrificial, the closer you go to the Spiritual Triad.

Once Buddha said, "I became a Buddha because I have served thousands of Buddhas in my many incarnations." Who are the Buddhas? They are those who are enlightened by the light of the Intuition or the Spiritual Triad. Buddhas are the pure Selves in each human being. If you serve the highest in each man and the highest Men, you slowly enter into the path of Buddhahood.

Thus the human soul enters into the Spiritual Triad, proceeds toward the Monad and eventually becomes a Thousand Petaled Lotus in full bloom, the petals of which are electromagnetic devices for communication with Higher Galaxies, Beings, Sources of Wisdom and Beauty, and Spheres of higher Direction and Purpose.

As your Self unfolds, gradually you lose your individual Self and you become one with the Cosmic Self.

When we speak about the Monad, people think we are referring to something separate.

Each Monad—the reflection of which is the human soul—is a focus of fire hung from a thread of fire projected by the All-Self. You, as a spider, come down to matter with your own thread and slowly go back through swallowing the same thread. You go step by step to your archetypes reflected on the forty-nine levels of Cosmos.

Thus our root is in the Cosmic Self, and we go back to our origin, in greater and greater glory. Each of us must not feel cut from our Source but feel that, in essence, we are continually tied to our Source.

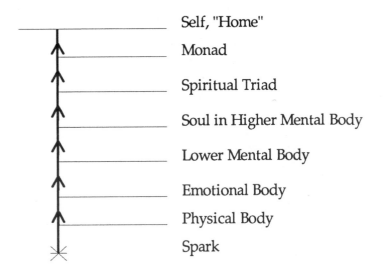

Self, "Home"

Monad

Spiritual Triad

Soul in Higher Mental Body

Lower Mental Body

Emotional Body

Physical Body

Spark

—— The Road Back Home ——

You reach the Self by leaving behind all that you built, you learned, and you did, through the line of life extended from the All-Self.

When you realize this, you no longer take time to play with spirits and entities; instead, you *work out* your own salvation with your own feet and hands.

All these achievements are accomplished through steady and continuous meditation, service, and self-denial.

Meditation is a science, and one must do meditation scientifically.

Service is a science, and one must know how to serve.

Self-denial is a science, and one must proceed on this path scientifically.

Meditation is divided into three sections: concentration, meditation, and contemplation.

Concentration is identification with the purpose that you have in your mind.

Meditation is a process of penetration into this purpose and into the steps leading you to the purpose.

Contemplation is fusion with the purpose through withdrawal from your lower selves into your ultimate Self.

What is the ego? The ego is the human soul identified with the vehicle he is in. Because of such an identification, part of the ego has involutionary tendencies which are separative and self-interested. When the ego is on the physical plane, he uses all that he has on the physical plane for his self, his separative interest. He does the same thing on the emotional plane. He uses all his emotions and feelings for self-interest. On the mental plane he uses all his knowledge and powers for self-interest.

When the ego detaches himself from his vehicles, he gradually lives as a human soul because he no longer continues to live for himself but for everything that exists.

The soul is evolutionary. The ego is in conflict between the pull of evolution and the pull of involution.

The ego slowly changes to the human soul by the following:

— Detaching from his vehicles

— Orienting himself toward his glorious future

— Demonstrating continuous sacrificial service

Psychics must continuously educate themselves. An advanced psychic told us one day in his lecture that every psychic must study:

1. *The Secret Doctrine* and *Isis Unveiled* by H. P. Blavatsky

2. *H.P. Blavatsky, Tulku and Tibet* by Geoffrey A. Barborka

3. *Damodar* by Sven Eek

4. All the books by Alice A. Bailey

5. Ouspensky

6. Gurdjieff

7. The Agni Yoga books

8. The *Bhagavad Gita*

9. The *Upanishads*

10. The books by Shankaracharya

11. The *I Ching*

12. The *Vishnu Puranas*

13. The *Vedas*

14. The *Lotus Sutra*

15. The *New Testament*

He said that "in the future a college of psychism will prepare lessons and classes on these books."

After one goes through such a study, he will know what true psychism is, what the dangers are, and how he can refine himself to be of greater service to humanity. Of course, the greatest study of a psychic will be in the "Book of Life and Experience."

A psychic must not be limited by what is given because more powerful psychics who will have the sense of synthesis will be born and will help the service of psychism advance to new heights.

— 4 —

The Human Soul

The human soul is a phase in the development of the Spark of divinity within us. The Self and the soul are almost the same. The Spark is the seed, the soul is the bud, and the Self is the full-bloomed flower.

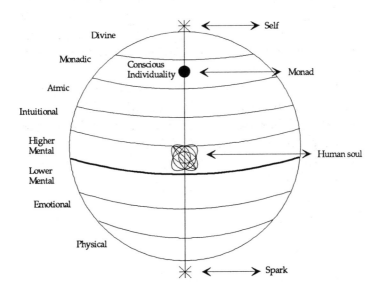

—— **Unfolding of the Spark** ——

The Spark is the reflection of the Monad, but at this stage of human life man is Spark, ego, or soul.

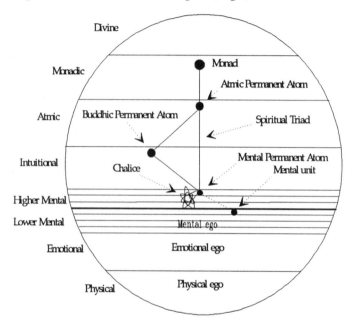

Divine

Monadic

Monad

Atmic Permanent Atom

Atmic   Buddhic Permanent Atom

Spiritual Triad

Intuitional   Chalice

Mental Permanent Atom
Mental unit

Higher Mental

Lower Mental   Mental ego

Emotional   Emotional ego

Physical   Physical ego

——— The Human Constitution ———

The Spark is growing into a soul, into the Monad, into Self-hood—just as the body is becoming a youth, an adult, and a full grown man. He is the same man, but he is passing through certain phases of development.

The Spark is the electricity in the body which causes all mechanical processes that make it possible for the body to grow and sustain its life. When the Spark travels, so to say, to the astral body, it begins to build and organize the astral body with its seven centers and seven senses.

When the Spark travels to the mental body, it develops "I am" consciousness and begins to think about itself as a separate being. This happens in the lower mental body. The Spark tries to organize the mental body and unfold its centers and senses and the other mechanisms in it.

We must remember that the Spark is programmed to go forward, and for ages and ages it waits for the formation of its bodies of communication.

When the Spark develops the consciousness that it is not the body, emotional or mental vehicles, it begins to travel to the higher mind. From there it learns to master its lower mind, emotional, and mental bodies. As it gains mastery over its bodies, in that degree it becomes a soul. Thus, the soul is the Spark living on the higher mental plane, with full control over its lower vehicles.

Ages later, as the human soul unfolds more, its light, love and power aspects penetrate into the Intuitional Plane and it forms a relationship with the Mental Permanent Atom, the Intuitional, and the Atmic Permanent Atoms and locates itself at the center of the energy field formed by the radiations of the three permanent atoms.

The physical body is a device for the human soul to contact the physical world. The astral body is a device built for the human soul to come in contact with the astral world. Not many people have an organized and well developed astral body. Some astral bodies are sick, paralyzed, amputated, frozen, even dead. A very few people have a healthy astral body that is not fully developed yet. Even fewer have fully developed astral bodies which are capable of relating the human soul to the astral world through its senses and centers.

Few people are aware of the astral world, not because it does not exist, but because they do not have mechanisms to come in contact with it.

Some people ooze out of their bodies and enter into the astral world consciously to study and observe it with their astral senses. They have firsthand experience of how dangerous that world is and of how many people blindly are captured by astral glamors.

To relate to the mental world, to be alive and in existence in the mental world, the soul tries to develop the mental mechanisms. Not many people can penetrate into the mental world. Such a penetration needs not only a well-developed mental body, but also all the senses in order to live in and understand the mental world. Once our mental body is developed, time and space slowly disappear.

Dreams are reflections in the astral plane of those happenings which are going on on higher or lower planes. But we are not aware of these events until our astral and mental consciousnesses are fully developed.

It is sometimes possible to penetrate into the mental plane, but it does not help us until we have developed our mental equipment fully. This is why it is necessary that psychics develop their mental bodies instead of involving themselves with various entities and spirits. The honesty and sincerity of the latter cannot be proved.

Man is the key to the Universe. Why depend on spirits or on so called "spirits in higher planes"? Even if they convey to us secret knowledge, we will not be able to translate and understand them because our bodies are not ready, and, if ready, we do not need them as we can individually contact sources of wisdom face to face in full consciousness.

People dream about standing on high rocks and falling down, or of burning in fire, drowning in water. During such dreams they experience these events as nightmares. Their astral or mental consciousness is still fused with the physical consciousness, and they think that their physical body fell down, burned, or drowned. Until we detach our astral and mental consciousness from the physical consciousness, we cannot be awake and consciously work on higher planes. This is what psychics must do.

In the astral and mental worlds, you will be as conscious as you are here. Self-actualization is the process of developing the consciousness of your existence in astral, mental, and higher planes.

The divinity within you must be able to function on all planes consciously. Man desires to have, man desires to know, man desires to do, but the greatest desire is *to be*. As you are on the physical plane, you must *be* also on higher planes.

Whatever you crave, you become that object. In becoming that object, you negate your True Self. You slander yourself.

You must develop a consciousness in which nothing belongs to you, in which the things that are given to you are given only to make you use them properly, without attachment. Only through *beingness* can you surpass all materialism, all knowingness, and all doingness. Beingness is the goal of every person who feels the call of the Cosmic Magnet.

On the higher mental plane the human soul, who is conscious of his individual existence, begins to prepare himself to climb higher levels of awareness by building a ladder to the Intuitional Plane, which is called the higher bridge. There is a difference between the human soul that is on the higher mental planes and the one that is in the lower mind. The soul in the lower mind is called an ego, a "soul" that is primarily occupied with his self-interest and pleasures. He is separative and likes to manipulate and exploit.

The soul on the higher mental plane is free of egotism and lives a life for the benefit of all that exists.

It takes many hundreds of incarnations for our ego to move from the lower mental plane to the higher mental plane. On the higher mental plane, you become divinely creative; you become a thinker and server. These are the outstanding characteristics of a human soul:

— The ability to think

— The ability to create

— The ability to serve

From the lower mental plane the human soul climbs to the higher mental plane.

As one proceeds to the higher mental plane, the human soul experiences more understanding, wisdom, patience, perseverance, solemnity, nobility, and truth.

As you advance in the higher mental body and perfectly organize your mental body, you can consciously withdraw from your physical and astral bodies and function in the sphere of the mental world of the Planetary Soul.

Here you are beginning to be a real psychic, a high level psychic, and the Divine Treasury is almost opening for you to enjoy pure knowledge and wisdom. In this stage you do not need astral or mental entities, spirits, etc., because you yourself can function consciously on higher planes.

After the soul penetrates into the Intuitional Plane, he slowly becomes a triangle—a diamond. His next station is Monad-hood, and the highest is Self-hood. A Self is an open window to the Self of the Cosmos.

On each step of our evolution the potentials of our inner divinity begin to manifest more and more.

Those people who die before they are souls enter into a sphere of unconscious existence, and the laws and forces of nature take the "soul" here and there, like a piece of wood on the ocean, then throw it to the shore of another incarnation. Such people start where they left off in their previous life. To be consciously alive in the subtle worlds, you must hurry and become a conscious soul.

People are not consciously immortal until they become conscious souls. Immortality is related to continuity of consciousness. People's consciousness stays the same; as on earth, so in Space after death. Our efforts must be directed to expand our consciousness so that we can enjoy this consciousness after death and during the process of our next incarnation.

The Solar Angel

We are told that eighteen million years ago, in Lemurian times, Great Beings came from one of the chains of the Venus scheme. They were divided into two parties. One of the parties was composed of *Kumaras*, one hundred and five of Them, Who established the Hierarchy on this planet.[1]

The second party was composed of millions and millions of Angels, Who were called *Nirvanis*. They came in three waves. The first wave came and observed the state of development of humanity and thought that humanity was not ready for the help They could give. But Their presence on earth created a better responsiveness.

The second wave came a thousand years later and, seeing the improved state of evolution of humanity, They put a piece of Their mental fire in the mental body of man, which was later used to build the Chalice or the body of the Solar Angel.

The third wave came and They anchored Themselves in the Chalice, in the mental body of man. These are called the Solar Angels.

The second wave left a precious mental substance in the mental body of man, which eventually developed into the Lotus—the Chalice—and became the anchorage of the Solar Angel. Human consciousness began

---

1. For further information, see *The Legend of Shamballa*, 2nd ed., by Torkom Saraydarian (Sedona: AZ, Aquarian Educational Group, 1988).

to develop from the date when the Solar Angels entered into the mental body of men.

Previously, man was a member of the human race, the soul of which was a Great Being. He was acting as a Group Soul, and every human being was living as a member of the body of the human race, just as unborn children live in their mother's womb.

When the Solar Angel came, the umbilical cord of each human being was cut from the mass consciousness, and the human being individualized. He consciously saw that he was an individual, not the mass.

It is assumed that the moment of individualization was the first moment when the sense of responsibility began in man. The sense of responsibility is the bridge which will carry individual consciousness to Group Consciousness.

When the Solar Angel entered into the third level of the human mental body many things happened.

1. Millions of people went berserk and died. This was a test of survival of the fittest. The energy was too much for these humans to handle.

2. Those who adjusted themselves began to advance and became leaders, teachers, and rulers.

3. Sex became divided into male and female.

4. A little light began to radiate in the mental body of man. That light was the beginning of the consciousness of the individualized person.

How did this happen?

Occultism says that the Solar Angel searched for the *human soul* and with a ray contacted him on whatever level he was. Then it pulled him up to higher levels of the mental plane and, fusing Its light with the human soul, evoked the intelligence aspect of the soul.

The human soul has (as also the Great Beings have) three aspects:

Light—Intelligence

Love

Willpower

The intelligence aspect of the human soul and the Solar Angel's fusing with it created that lighted field which is called the *consciousness of man.*

It is the consciousness that gradually made him aware

1. that the person was a separate being

2. that things exist outside of him

3. that he can keep the memory of his contact with objects outside of him

4. that he can think for tomorrow

5. that he can see the relation of cause and effect

6. that he can plan

7. that he can compare and differentiate

8. that he can formulate his thoughts in speech

9. that he can organize

10. that he can have goals

As his relation with the Solar Angel increased, the light of his consciousness increased and he developed these ten qualities in their higher and higher correspondences. These are the signs of human consciousness.

To repeat, every human soul has three aspects:

Light—Intelligence

Love

Willpower

The Solar Angel evoked the intelligence aspect of the human soul to start the light of the consciousness. The light is the result of the radiation of the human soul on the mental plane. The Solar Angel will then evoke the love aspect, then the will aspect.

Each of us has the love and will aspects in potentiality, not in manifestation yet. It is the Solar Angel who will evoke the love and willpower.

In the Fourth Initiation the three aspects will reach higher states of development and harmony which will cause a man to be an Arhat. So the consciousness will be qualified by

Light—with intelligence

Love—with compassion

Willpower—with beauty

In the Fifth Initiation these three must reach a very high state of development to enable man to pass the tests of the Fifth Initiation.

Let us remember that there is

1. A Group Solar Angel

2. A National Solar Angel

3. The Solar Angel of Humanity, which is the Hierarchy

4. The Solar Angel of Earth, which is Venus

5. The Solar Angel of the Solar System, which is a magnificent Star

The Solar Angel is an Initiate of all degrees. It is always in contact with the Lord of Shamballa. It is a reporter. It reports all that goes on in our life.

Our Angels see the face of the Father, the Ancient of Days, every day. If we understand the implication of this statement, we realize how important it is to live a noble life, a life that is a sacrificial service throughout.

Because of the Solar Angel's compassion, It stays with us for ages until we graduate from the school of this planetary life.

Of course, our Solar Angel is also a Traveler on the Path like us, though It is millions of years more advanced that we are. It has Its divine duties and responsibilities. It also has Its lessons to learn in galactic universities.

Every time the Solar Angel is baby-sitting us, It is also "reading books" and may be watching events going on in Cosmos.

In the Universe there is no end to achievement. Every atom, every life on earth or in space, is progressing ahead toward Infinity. Life has no beginning and no end.

— 6 —

Higher Psychics

There is always a great need for political leaders, doctors, lawyers, and artists. But the greatest need is for higher psychics who are able scientifically to contact Higher Spheres of light and leadership and bring them to the world of men in the form of

- new rules

- new laws

- new inspirations

- new directions

- new ideas

to guide the steps of leaders in all fields.

In the ancient world, every leader was guided by a true psychic, or he himself was a psychic. If you study the history of great leaders in the world, you will find a psychic behind them. Most of them were consulted in secret, some of them openly. This is the case even today.

Some psychics lead leaders in the right direction; some in the wrong direction. Leaders are led in the right direction when the psychic is of high quality as, for example, a high quality surgeon.

High quality means that the psychic is

1. Pure physically, emotionally, and mentally

2. In contact at least with the Intuitional Plane

3. Knows the language of Higher Spheres

4. Is protected from interferences

Every higher psychic is a target of dark forces.
Higher psychism is accepted by the Hierarchy and functions according to the Plan and the Law of Karma.
Low level psychics are controlled

1. By etheric entities

2. By astral entities

3. By lower mental entities

4. By astral corpses

5. By impure physical, emotional, and mental bodies, glamors, illusions, and personal interests

Such psychics have no access beyond the lower mental planes, and they are not accepted by Hierarchy. Such psychics, who most of the time are low mediums, not only deceive people but also deceive themselves.

The future of higher psychics is entrance into greater usefulness.

The future of lower psychics is obsession, possession, pain, and suffering.

People think that all psychic potentials must be cultivated by practicing special yogas, by working on chakras, centers, by using drugs, doing breathing exercises, by necromancy, etc.

Of course, these methods can prematurely and artificially open certain potentials but bring disasters in the future. The safest methods are given by Great Ones as follows:

1. Sacrificial service

    a. to enlighten people

    b. to heal and feed people

    c. to free people

    d. to increase joy in people

    e. to lead people into cooperation and synthesis

2. Scientific meditation to come in contact with the Divine Mind

3. Building continuity of consciousness

Psychic powers must not be developed artificially through

    a. drugs

    b. breathing exercises

    c. Hatha Yoga

    d. concentrating upon centers or upon ganglias

They must be flowers of age-long labor, service, and expansion of consciousness.

Every true psychic power, or release of an inner potential, is the result of

sacrificial service

meditation

harmlessness

Sacrificial service, meditation, and harmlessness create a karma which eventually makes a person worthy for the blooming of his inner potentials.

What are these Higher Inner Potentials?

— Ability to come in contact with *archetypes*

— Ability to see the Future

— Ability to cooperate with the Plan

— Ability to work with the members of Hierarchy

— Ability to love unconditionally

Whenever love is not sacrificial, and imposition and fanaticism are in power, the spirit dies and the body takes over.

How can you refine your psychic powers and use them as tools to serve humanity? Some of you may be in contact with Higher Beings. Some of you are in contact with astral entities or astral corpses. Some of you are in contact with charlatans and liars from the etheric plane.

Some of you have contact with Angels.

Some of you are in contact with your Inner Guide, your Solar Angel.

Some of you are under the attack of dark forces.

Some of you are fooled by jokers or amusers. There are certain devas which enjoy playing with human beings and deceiving them.

It is a grave and dangerous experience to have such contacts.

The questions we must ask are these:

1. How to be masters of our communication?

2. How to advance in our communication?

3. How to surpass those who communicate with us?

4. How to find higher sources of communication?

The answer to all of these questions is *to build continuity of consciousness*.[1]

What are the preparatory steps?

Physical—exercise, such as various sports, hiking, climbing mountains, swimming.

Emotional—dispassion, detachment, love, gratitude, and silence. Non-reaction to fear, anger, hatred, jealousy, revenge, treason.

Mental—concentration, regular meditation, contemplation, illumination, and a proper field of labor and service.

We serve humanity from the level we are on. Our service to humanity is what we are. Our service to

---

1. For further information regarding the Rainbow Bridge, please refer to the following books by Torkom Saraydarian: *The Psyche and Psychism, The Science of Becoming Oneself,* and *The Science of Meditation* (Agoura, CA: Aquarian Educational Group, 1981).

humanity is what we can give. This means that our service is equal to

    1. our beingness

    2. our knowingness

    3. our level and focus of consciousness

Psychic powers start in animals and progress to Angels. For example, certain insects, fish, birds, and other animals have "psychic powers."

Some human beings have psychic powers. These psychic powers are given

    1. By the Group Soul

    2. By certain entities

    3. By your Soul in critical times

    4. As the result of ages of development

Senses and centers on all levels are psychic senses. There are

    Physical senses

    Astral senses

    Mental senses

When the senses of the bodies and their corresponding centers are open, we witness psychic powers. There are also Intuitional senses and centers which, when unfolded in a man, that man becomes an Arhat. When the Atmic senses and centers are open, a man becomes a Master.

The higher your psychism is, the closer you are to your True Self.

If your psychism is astral, you are

> in deception

> in a destructive mood

> in negativity

> involved in personality interests

If your consciousness is lower mental, you have

> greed

> separatism

> ego

> vanity

> illusion

If you are focused on the higher mental plane, you dedicate yourself to

> service

> inclusiveness

> simplicity and clarity

> sacrifice

Intuitional psychism surpasses all psychic powers of the lower planes.

How to advance:

1. Do not depend on astral entities, so-called guides, masters, and the like.

2. Depend on your reason and logic

3. Develop thinking

4. Build the antahkarana

5. Study

6. Meditate

7. Serve

8. Develop psychic energy [2]

Depending on any entity, spirit, or "master" hinders your progress. You are going to unfold the beauty, power, treasure, and glory hidden within you. Perfection must be achieved by the labor done on yourself.

The most noble life is a life dedicated to service for humanity. The greatest person is a person who renders the greatest service to humanity.

There are many ways to serve humanity, but, again, the greatest way to serve humanity is to serve the soul of humanity. This is what the service of a true psychic is. To serve the soul of people means seven things:

1. To cultivate in man an invincible urge toward beauty

2. To release in man the power of goodness

3. To release in man the light of righteousness

4. To reveal to man the real meaning of freedom

5. To release in man the inner source of joy

6. To educate man to understand the power of gratitude

7. To prepare man for a life of sacrificial service

2. For further information on this topic, refer to *A Commentary on Psychic Energy* (West Hills, CA: T.S.G. Enterprises, 1989) by Torkom Saraydarian.

These are the seven lights that a true psychic uses to enlighten souls.

What is a psychic? The purest definition of a psychic is this: *A psychic is a person who increasingly demonstrates the powers of his soul and uses them for the service of humanity.*

What are the powers of the human soul?

1. Ability to function on the physical, astral, and mental planes of existence simultaneously

2. Ability to pass beyond these three planes without losing continuity of consciousness and to be active in the Intuitional sphere

3. Ability to communicate with the "rain clouds of wisdom"

4. Ability to attend subjective Ashrams

5. Ability to have interviews with one's Master

6. Ability to withdraw from the threefold personality

7. Ability to study Akashic records by permission

8. Ability to protect people from dark attacks

In the future we will have universities to teach these eight fields and produce a true psychic.

In true psychism the emphasis is laid on the expansion of consciousness, which is the focus of consciousness from level to level with *continuity*.

In higher psychism, man does not depend on entities or spirit guides; he develops himself.

7

Self-Actualization

The greatest purpose in our life is to bring into manifestation and operation the hidden Divinity within us. All life forms, from an atom to a galaxy, have the same purpose: To manifest the concealed Divinity within themselves.

This concealed Divinity manifests as beauty, health, happiness, prosperity, abundance, wisdom, and as higher psychic powers. Psychic manifestations are evolutionary in the lower kingdoms, but in man and in higher forms of life, such manifestations are the result of a conscious act. Man cooperates with that concealed glory and, through his striving, lets that glory manifest. It is also possible that man lives in a way that this process of manifestation of Inner Divinity slows down or is not actualized for centuries or lives.

Our greatest labor is to bring that Inner Divinity into our daily life and relationships, with all its richness and beauty.

The major characteristics of the Self are

1. All-inclusiveness

2. Attunement with the Supreme Purpose of the Central Core of the Universe

3. Isolated unity

4. Everlasting beingness through all temporary forms

5. Omniscience

6. Omnipresence

7. Omnipotence

8. Independence

All-inclusiveness is the first characteristic of the Self. The closer you get to your True Self, the more you become inclusive in your thinking, feelings, and activities. This means that separation on all levels of your personality disappears. You begin to see your identity with the essence of every living form. Separation is not only the source of all vices, but also the source of all pain and suffering and ignorance.

All that you think, feel, and do against inclusiveness works against the major purpose of your life, so you must be very careful not to serve the devil of separatism but through your whole life actualize the spirit of inclusiveness.

All-inclusiveness does not mean to bring together gasoline and fire, to invite a rattlesnake into your home, to bring together poison and food, ugliness and beauty, evil and good. It is not a separative act if you refuse to have sex with one who has AIDS. It is not a separative act when you lock up an insane criminal or an insane person, or if you refuse to cooperate in business with a person whose intention is to cheat you.

All-inclusiveness means

1. To recognize the right of every Spark to manifest its Divinity the way it wants

2. To give every Spark the opportunity to bloom

3. To feel happy for the success and happiness of every Spark

4. To exercise compassion toward every form of life and realize that in essence you are one with them

5. To be tolerant, understanding, and forgiving

6. To serve and sacrifice in order to make others advance

7. Not to lose the opportunity to cooperate with those who are on the path of transformation or engaged in constructive labor

8. To exercise the power of synthesis which helps you approach people and problems from as many viewpoints as possible

9. To have an urge to unite and create unity and linkage between units having the goal of universal unity

These characteristics are within your Core, and if you work against them you create karma.

The second characteristic is *attunement with the Supreme Purpose of the Central Core of the Universe.* There is that note within each of us which is in resonance always with that Cosmic Purpose. That is your supreme guidance, your star leading you Home. In your higher moments you feel it, and this feeling charges your soul with powerful bliss and joy, but often your brain and logic cannot translate the meaning of such a resonance, which is the link between the Source and you. It is this Source that gives you *direction*. Humanity would be lost ages ago if it did not have such a link with Cosmic Direction.

The realization of such a link is a supreme ecstasy for your whole being. You are not lost in the Universe but the beacon is there, within you, to guide you Home.

Moments of realization of the resonance are the moments of contemplation, the moments of bliss and freedom in a higher sense. Every time you feel this resonance, you feel the Universal Core reverberating within your being. Daily you must try in your own way to tune yourself in to that Cosmic note.

Isolated unity is the third characteristic. You are one with every form, in essence, and are not attached to any form. You are one with the spirit, but you are detached from the forms or bodies of that spirit. Thus, you protect yourself from problems of the form side of the spirit, but help the form through its spiritual part.

You advance on the ladder of unity in spirit and detach from all forms. Thus, you are detached but also united in essence. This characteristic is within you and needs actualization.

The next characteristic is *everlasting beingness through all temporary forms.* Immortality or persistent existence is your heritage. You are a part of the Almighty Presence which was, is, and will be in all forms through which you lived and passed out of, but you still exist, in greater consciousness and with greater powers. Temporary forms are vehicles that you have had in many kingdoms throughout your evolution. They pass, but you *die not.* Actually, you never die and you never are born—*you are.* You exist through all "nights and days."

Omniscience is another characteristic of your True Self. It means that you know everything. Knowledge is the Great Presence in the Universe, and you are part of It. You need only to contact and be your Self and you will know all that is there through Self-actualization, which is bringing out all wisdom that is hidden in the Core of the Self.

A day will come when we will not need to learn because the Cosmic Knowledge hidden within our Core will manifest itself in our mental and Intuitional Planes.

Purification of our vehicles will lead us to the treasury of that wisdom. When Plato said, "Learning is remembering," he revealed a great secret.

Actually, what are we doing in listening to high level lectures and reading various books? We are stirring the treasury of our Inner Divinity so that this treasury precipitates upon our mental plane, and we see in the mirror of our mind, things that exist within our Core. The Self knows everything. We need only to penetrate into our own Core.

Holiness leads us toward our Self because, in its real meaning, holiness is a process of becoming one's Self, gradually leaving behind all that is not Self, within and without. Purity eventually makes our Inner Sun radiate out with all Its glory.

Whatever you learn from your own Self will remain with you through Infinity. Whatever you learn from those who have no Self-contact, eventually will be unlearned if you want to penetrate into true knowledge.

Omnipresence is the sixth characteristic. You in your essence are everywhere, in everything, as a part of the One Self. This can be actualized by expanding your love and compassion. The more love you have, the more space you occupy.

Omnipotence is the seventh characteristic. The whole power of the Creative Source is in you. You need only to find the keys to enter into that power-house.

Independence is the eighth characteristic. Independence is the power of the spirit to conquer the involutionary tendencies of all its vehicles, the involutionary currents of all forces, and to forge ahead on its path toward home without being trapped by any living form, by any spirit or entity.

Independence is the most powerful tendency in man. It is a tendency to avoid being manipulated and used by any entity whose intention is to limit your freedom and obstruct the path leading to your True Self.

Thoughts, words, feelings, and actions against these eight potent characteristics of the Self create powerful karma in our earth life.

Actualization is of three kinds:

1. *Actualization of blueprints or archetypes.* Archetypes are those electrical forms which are created by the Cosmic Mind. Our duty is to bring them into manifestation in political, educational, philosophic, artistic, scientific, religious, and economic fields. They are the blueprints of all human activities and creativity. Just as you give a blueprint to your builder and ask him to build a house according to it, there are blueprints in Space which have been waiting for ages for actualization through human endeavors.

For example, how many centuries have passed while human beings advanced from the oil lamp to the modern forms of light? How many thousands of years passed while people stopped using a donkey for travel and used, instead, the modern jets or space shuttles? Blueprints are seeds of future glorious achievements.

Another archetype is to make yourself like Christ, the perfect archetypical man, a full bloomed perfection. Such an archetype is waiting for all of us, and life after life we are trying to get closer to His "measures," inch by inch. "Gods" must eventually walk on earth.

The model is within us: the most beautiful, immortal body; the purest emotions; the most efficient mind; the most victorious soul which can master form, energy, space, and time.

There are other archetypes, for example: archetypes of groups, nations, relationships, family; archetypes of sacred conditions, of cooperation.

2. *Actualization of latent potentials.* The second form of actualization is to bring into manifestation all our latent potentials. For example, all our senses have their archetypes which, when actualized, will give us Cosmic contact on all planes.

This is the symbol of a potential in process of actualization. This archetype takes millions of years to manifest, and every hundred years some people actualize two percent of it. In the next century they actualize eight percent. Another two thousand years passes, and some human beings become able to manifest the potential in its full beauty.

Actualization starts from the physical plane and goes to the highest, the Divine Plane, on each plane revealing a new aspect of the archetype. The archetype of all our potentials will one day unfold to its full bloom.

We have so much to do "to be perfect, as our Father is perfect," if only we pull our nose out of matter, self-interest, greed, hate, and so on.

We have seven potentials, and these potentials must manifest and actualize eventually in our lives. Each one of us has these seven potentials.

1.   Power of Rulership

2.   Power of Enlightenment

3.   Power of Communication

4.   Power of Creativity and Beauty

5.   Power of Knowing

6.   Power of Contacting Almighty Beings

7.   Power of Sharing

All these potentials must manifest in their full beauty because each of them has its archetype.

For example, in ancient China Confucius gave instructions for leaders, kings, officers, fathers, mothers, children, and so on, on how to behave, how to relate to each other. His purpose was to reveal archetypes of proper conduct. Thus, he tried to bring all human relationships into their archetypical beauty.

All life forms are parts of one great archetype which is unfolding through them, carrying them toward perfection. This is evolution. Evolution is the process of actualization of divine archetypes. Of course, human free will can fight for ages against archetypes and bring suffering and pain upon itself.

3. *Actualization of your Inner Divinity*. The third kind of actualization is not only to unfold your hidden potential or to actualize divine archetypes, but also to manifest the Divinity that you are in your essence.

These three actualizations are like three sides of an equilateral triangle. They grow together and support each other in every step of your evolution.

Some Exercises for Self-actualization

These exercises are very beneficial for your health and happiness. Do them in a very relaxed and happy mood.

Exercise One

1. Sit relaxed and be happy.

2. Concentrate your consciousness at the middle point inside your head.

3. Visualize leaving your body on the chair and go to a garden.

4. Sit in the garden and think about your body.

5. Come back near your body and observe it from the

front
back
right
left
above

Take your time and observe it calmly.

6. Stand five feet in front of your body and send a beam of violet light from your forehead to the places of your body which need healing or energizing. Do not let the beam of light stay long on one location. This process must not exceed 60 seconds total.

7. Go back to the garden and relax.

8. Dance in the garden to nice music.

9. Come back and repeat number six.

10. Enter into your body.

After you are in the body, rub your hands together, touch your face, and slowly open your eyes. Record your experiences.

Exercise Two

1. Visualize a building having three rooms.

2. The first room is violet in color; the second room blue; the third room orange, with a small window.

3. Go toward the building and lie down in front of it. Leave your physical body and enter into

the first room with your etheric body. Notice the color of the first room.

4. Leave your etheric body in the first room, enter into the second, the blue room, with your astral body.

5. Leave your astral body behind and enter into the orange colored room with your mental body. Sit and visualize your physical-etheric and astral bodies. Leave your mental body and, like a five pointed star, go into space as a soul.

6. Feel how free you are. Circle around the globe and enjoy the speed and freedom.

7. Come back through the window and heal your mental body from sicknesses such as greed, vanity, ego, separatism, illusion. See these sicknesses as black spots and annihilate them with a beam of psychic energy coming from the center of the star.

8. Do the same thing with your astral body, healing certain gray matter in it which is hate, anger, fear, jealousy, revenge, slander, malice, treason.

9. Do the same thing with your etheric body, healing it from inertia, exhaustion, revitalizing the seven chakras at once.

10. Do the same thing with your physical body, but this time be slow and cure all that needs to be cured or corrected in the physical body.

11. Go back to the mental body and put it on.

12. Do the same thing with the astral body.

13. Do the same thing with the etheric body.

14. Do the same thing with your physical body.

Rub your hands together, touch your face, and sit for a few minutes and relax.

Exercise Three

To protect ourselves from attacks, the following can be considered.

1. Visualize a fiery, five pointed star and stand at the center of it.

2. Try to recognize your glamors and not identify with them.

3. Try to use your spiritual will, evoking it through your Solar Angel or the Hierarchy.

NOTE

These are powerful exercises. Do them with the permission of your medical doctor. They can be used every other day with excellent results.

Factors in Self-actualization

There are five factors in Self-actualization:

1. All that exists are parts of a complete whole.

2. Every part of the whole affects the other parts.

3. The innermost urge of every part is to become a conscious part of the whole.

4. The essential urge of every part is to be the whole.

5. The mystery to be solved is how to be the whole without depriving all parts of the consciousness that they are also the whole.

Each disciple, Initiate, and leader on the Path does not have a more sacred duty than to

— analyze

— understand

— be

— formulate paths

for every kind of person to enter the road of absolute unity.

The Path is trodden by five steps:

— The first portion of the Path is the path of "I desire."

— Then, "I want to collect and accumulate."

— Then, "I want to know."

— Then, "I want to be."

— Finally, "I want to serve."

On all levels—physically, emotionally, mentally— we see these five steps. Once our consciousness enters into the Intuitional Plane, the only two urges that we see existing are *to be* and *to serve.*

Service is the scientific technique that leads to the path of unification on all levels, but one needs to *BE* in order to be able to *SERVE.*

Service is the process of sharing your beingness. Beingness is the flower of age-long experience and discipline.

8

Mediumship and Higher Worlds

The Ageless Wisdom is against necromancy. It warns against mediumistic activities and warns the servers and students to stay away from all sciences of materialization, channeling, or automatic writing.

Mediums are in contact with shells or, as they are called in esoteric science, corpses, the "spirits" left on the astral plane.

What is an astral corpse? It is the astral body which the human soul leaves behind after he passes into the mental plane, or it is a mental corpse which the human soul leaves behind when he passes into higher mental realms.[*]

Thus, we have astral corpses which are of two kinds:

a. Those which last for a long time, according to the earthly and crude substances existing in it, such as lust, addictions, habits, etc.

b. Those which last a few months, days or hours. These are the corpses of very advanced human souls. Upon their departure to the Fiery World, their corpses begin to burn either slowly or quickly, or they explode immediately.

We also have mental corpses, which exist in two forms:

---

[*] Author's note: There are cases in which some Great Ones store their Higher Bodies for later use.

a. Those which melt away immediately and disappear.

b. Those which last a long time according to the earthbound thoughtforms of greed, possession, revenge, and guilt.

All those corpses that last for a long time in the subtle plane have a tendency to be attracted by the sphere of earth due to existing substances in them of hatred, anger, fear, jealousy, revenge, malice, slander, etc., and due to the existence of ego, vanity, separatism, illusion, greed, revenge, and so on.

Mediums are those who give such corpses energy to come closer to human life and thus reactivate them.

How do the mediums reactivate them?

Ectoplasm and astral energy ooze out of the mediums, building a link between the medium and the corpse, and the impressions existing within the centers and senses of the corpse begin to play back, as if they were tapes or diskettes.

The subconscious mind and sometimes the conscious mind of the medium put the corpse in action and draw the "answers" that the medium needs or messages that he expects, thus making him think that he is in contact with a departed soul.

According to the Ageless Wisdom, no departed souls (except those who are caught in the etheric plane) can come down to earth. But the medium's soul can go into the Subtle Worlds, and if he is trained, he can come in contact with departed ones. But if he is not trained, he associates himself with their corpses, thinking that they are living entities.

In spiritualistic seances, the apparitions are nothing else but the condensation of a corpse, vested and activated by the ectoplasm of the medium.

It is possible that an advanced psychic may come in contact with living Teachers existing in Their etheric or physical bodies on the planet. This is very possible and such an advanced psychic can bring a great amount of wisdom from such Teachers.

It is also possible that some advanced psychics may come in contact with higher Hierarchies existing on sacred planets, for example, on Venus, where the source of the science of our planet is found. But to be able to contact Masters on Venus, one must have the purest heart possible for a human being.

Some mental corpses are identified with large amounts of scientific knowledge as well as other specialized knowledge. But that knowledge is not any more advanced than knowledge that had already registered in their mind while they were on earth. So these mediums who contact them gain nothing special. Mediums who do not have knowledge of contemporary science, for example, may think these corpses are giving something special!

Also, it is possible that these mental or astral corpses belong to preachers of various religions, and common-place preaching is received containing no wisdom that surpasses that of the past.

Future psychics will be trained not to make contact with shells or corpses, but to withdraw from their astral, lower mental, and even from their higher mental bodies and bypass corresponding astral and mental planes and come in contact with those enlightened spirits who live on the Intuitional Plane. Once such a contact is established consciously, the world will be blessed by a true science, by a true leadership for the good of all living forms on the planet.

What are the dangers of communicating with corpses?

a. Corpses bring astral and mental viruses into the bodies of mediums.

b. They degenerate a medium's immune system.

c. They bring confusion into the medium's mind and cause disorderliness in their lives.

d. They bring separatism, hatred, anger, revolutions, and war into humanity.

e. They agitate the minds of those with whom they had problems in the past.

f. They prevent people from striving for spiritual independence.

g. They spread lies and cause people and nations to stand against each other.

h. They pollute the aura of the medium and the aura of those who are around the medium.

i. Sometimes these corpses even come and melt into the astral and mental bodies of the mediums or into the people close to them, creating incurable mental and astral diseases.

j. These corpses can send signals to dark forces and provide astral or mental substance for them, allowing them to possess mediums and use them as agents of destruction, murder, and widespread crimes.

Those communities who tolerate mediumism eventually pay a high price for it in various ways.

We must bear in mind that our goal as human beings is to advance to Higher Worlds using the following five steps:

1. Continuous efforts with rigorous courses of study

2. Meditation

3. Harmlessness

4. Purity

5. Sacrificial service

The ascent of spirit or of the human soul toward higher dimensions is conditioned by the "weight" of his bodies, so to say.

The astral body and the mental body can be heavily loaded, or filled with substance that helps to move them toward higher directions.

What are these heavy "weights"?

1. Earthbound urges and drives such as excessive food, alcohol, drugs, sex, and attachment to property.

2. Negative emotions such as fear, anger, hatred, jealousy, revenge, cruelty, slander, malice, glamor.

3. Dense thoughtforms such as greed, vanity, ego, separatism, fanaticism, insincerity, wounds, and scars collected upon our subtle

bodies through harmful thoughts, words, and actions taken against others.

Such loads, wounds, and scars make it extremely difficult for a soul to ascend.

Some of these loads are inflammable materials which explode when passing through certain layers or frequencies of the astral and mental planes. In such cases, the human soul can have an experience of being in hell.

On the other hand, if the bodies of the human soul are filled with spiritual substance, it not only makes the flight easy but also an enjoyable journey.

The most precious "substance" of course is the psychic energy, which not only protects the human soul from various attacks but also opens the gates, so to say, on the Path and makes the human soul enjoy the bliss of freedom.

We have the substance of joy and compassion. We also have the substance which is called *hur*.* *Hur* comes into being and fills the centers of the subtle bodies every time a person engages himself in sacrificial service.

Another substance which is called *shogh** comes into being every time man renounces himself and thinks as a part of the One Self.

All virtues increase precious substances in our subtle bodies.

Meditation and evening review increase and store such substances. Filled with such substances, the human soul does not lose his Solar Angel and follows Its steps toward his destination.

---

* In Armenian *hur* means divine fire; *shogh* means ray. Ed.

Many human souls cannot follow the speed of their Solar Angels due to their burden, and every time they lose the Solar Angel, they merge into darkness.

This being the case, the souls who are advancing toward the Higher Worlds—except those who are trapped on the etheric plane—cannot be brought back, neither by spiritualists nor by those who use necromancy nor by mediums, channels, and lower psychics. The only possible way to contact them is to ascend to the spheres of the departed ones.

We must mention that when we die in one world, we are born in the next. For example, when we die on the physical plane, we are born on the astral plane. When we die on the astral plane, we are born on the mental plane.

It is only persons of the Fourth Initiation who can go beyond the mental.

The birth in the astral plane or mental plane does not give us new bodies but a new consciousness, which is a part of our consciousness but enlightened by new conditions.

For a short time, after every birth, the past is forgotten and then remembered. In the case of advanced Initiates, there is always continuity of consciousness.

These are the reasons why those who appear in seance rooms are not human beings but their corpses. Some people argue and say, for example, "But I have firsthand experience that my brother or father or wife appeared to me, or came to my dream and told me secrets that I did not know, and I can verify that all was the truth."

All these are possible. Those who are advanced in this occult science know that the astral centers and mental centers in the astral and mental corpses have all the recordings of life, but these recordings need a transmitting station to come in contact with people living in their physical bodies. The transmitting station is the image in the mind of the one who is to be contacted. Through this transmitting station, the information of the corpse reaches the brain of the subject. The following diagram simplifies this.

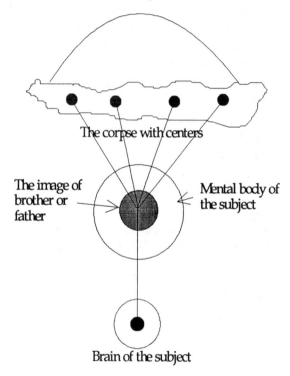

The corpse with centers

The image of brother or father

Mental body of the subject

Brain of the subject

There is also another possibility. When the image in the mind of the subject is highlighted by an intense aspiration, it can act as a transmission station between the Akashic Records and his brain, and the medium thinks that really a dead brother or father or mother is contacting him to pass over a secret. When the message is coming from the corpse, you see that it becomes more and more confusing as time goes by. Contact with Akashic Records does not bring full information because, first of all, a medium cannot stand the presence of it. Second, the transmission becomes intersected by other currents, unless the one who contacts the records has a very strong psychic mechanism of reception.

A person brought me a poem given to him by the "spirit" of Kahlil Gibran. After I read it, I gave the person *The Prophet* to read to see how inferior the poem was that he had received from the "spirit" and said, "Kahlil Gibran has been dead for fifty years. Don't you think that in fifty years his soul could give something far superior than what he gave on earth when he was alive?"

This is a very interesting phenomena. As the corpse begins to disintegrate, its memory becomes more confused, stupid, and foggy.

Mediums and others who call down the spirits of the dead are in grave danger. Here are some reasons:

1. The vices and subtle sicknesses of the corpse may take root in the medium's nature.

2. The elementals of the corpse may penetrate into the medium's aura, creating very complicated psychological disorders.

3. The corpses may disintegrate in the medium's home and environment, causing malodors and even burning the medium's skin.

4. The corpses can retard the medium's spiritual evolution, infecting his body with inertia, apathy, and degeneration.

5. The corpses can also sap all the vital energy of the person and kill the immune system.

There are honest and pure mediums. They give something worthwhile to people. But they do not know that they are in contact with their Solar Angel, or telepathically in contact with an advanced disciple.

Such mediums must be educated and trained so that gradually they make better and conscious contacts with their Solar Angels, and eventually stand face to face with Them.

It is only after the wisdom of the Solar Angel is assimilated and actualized that a true living Master comes in contact with a medium to convey the plan of His labor on earth. This is why advanced disciples must exercise tolerance and try to educate people who are sincerely devoted to communicating with higher sources of wisdom.

The advanced disciples must also cultivate compassion toward mediums and show them the dangers of mediumism, the dangers of lies and imitations.

Some very clever and gifted persons, to create attention toward themselves, pretend they are mediums and write books that are below average in quality. Through such an act they prostitute their talents and give the impression to the public that "spirits" exist and the proof is in their books or writings received from such spirits.

To bring such people to their senses is very difficult. But a true disciple must find ways to make the victim know that one day his false personality must be destroyed in order to make him free. It should be pointed out that such a destruction may take ages, leaving a medium behind in his spiritual evolution.

Most of our relationships with the world are maintained through our physical body. After death, as our physical body fades, our attachment to the physical world becomes less and less and our relationship with physical objects totally fades away. But because we still have emotional bodies, we feel emotional ties. When the emotional body leaves, the emotional ties disappear. But mental ties still exist. Mental ties are very few. For example, such ties are a result of activities based on creativity, great projects or plans for the future of humanity. But when the mental body passes away, such ties also vanish.

The only ties that remain are the ties between the soul and his Master, duties given by the Hierarchy and accepted, and missions accomplished in the world. The human soul has these ties if he was in contact with his Master, Hierarchy, with his Solar Angel, or if he had been able to accept a mission. But he also has ties in this stage with all his true co-workers, no matter where they exist in the vast Universe.

Mediums are persons who are mostly in contact with left-over astral shells, thoughtforms, or images of living or disembodied souls. The moment the human soul leaves his body, he has no interest in the physical objects except if he is trapped in the etheric plane.

A medium very easily can come in contact with such people and be poisoned by them because, actually, the etheric plane is the subtle physical plane. The inhabitants of this plane are all earthbound people. The medium provides them the substance to come in contact with the dense physical plane. Then a medium commits one of the greatest crimes in encouraging such souls not to penetrate into higher spheres and continue their cycle of evolution.

The inhabitants of this plane are
— murderers
— suicides
— materialists
— total unbelievers

A medium may have certain personal interests to be in contact with these sorts of inhabitants, but nothing is accomplished except that he hurts himself and he encourages such souls to stay longer in that plane.

A question arises: Suppose we have a great scientist who does not believe in life after death. If he is going to live in the etheric plane, can we profit by the knowledge which still exists in his etheric brain?

The answer is yes. Such a person will most probably stay for a long time in the etheric plane. Yes, we can profit from his knowledge, but what is the quality of a knowledge which has no vision of immortality in it? If the major goal of life is ignored, how can one develop faith in the knowledge or information received from such a soul? How can one profit from such a knowledge which is generated by material interests, hate, ego, separatism, and remains an end in itself?

Also, how will we be able to see the motivating power behind such a revealed knowledge?

We may wonder how long such a soul remains on the etheric plane. The time is not known, though it acts under precise laws. Such people will probably incarnate and have another chance to come in contact with their Solar Angel or with the light of a Master. It is possible that those who still live on earth can awaken them with their prayers and meditation and awaken in them the light of the eternal Path and lead them to the astral plane.

Some invisible helpers do just such a job. They may be taken by some ignorant mediums as the spirits of the departed ones. Invisible servers do not talk about the advanced Teaching, but they encourage, console, and bring understanding and peace to those with whom they communicate.

It is also possible that some mediums meet the souls of advanced disciples in astral or mental realms and think that they are in contact with spirits.

One of my friends was an expert in out-of-body activities. One day a medium came and told me that she was receiving messages from a "spirit" and she gave me a transcript of a message. I gave the message to my friend for evaluation. He smiled and put it on the table. The next time I took him another message, he took it and put it again on the table but this time he gave me a paper which was discussing the same topic in a better way than the medium's message. After I read it he asked, "What do you think?" "I think," I said, "you are her spirit." "Yes," he answered, "while I am in the Subtle World, she tunes in with me and receives ideas in a mixed form, thinking that I am a spirit."

So we have many sources from which a medium can receive messages. They are

- Corpses

- Dark forces

- Disembodied spirits

- Advanced disciples

- Their own egos

Some trance mediums leave their body and wander in astral or lower mental planes. This is considered very dangerous for the medium because not only does he separate himself from the body but also from his Solar Angel. This is very dangerous because, first, the vacated body can be possessed by certain entities, and the medium's mental body can fall into their control.

Second, the Solar Angel becomes dissatisfied with the trance medium's action and may stay detached or leave the trance medium for a short or a long time or forever. The Solar Angel does not like to live in such conditions.

During sleep the Solar Angel protects the human soul and, if possible, leads him to places where he can learn or serve. He does not like the person to be occupied with astral or mental corpses or disembodied entities.

Some of the trance mediums are in contact with thoughtforms of many Masters, Initiates, or Leaders which have been built by human creative imagination and visualization. Such thoughtforms are built with the help of millions of people to such a degree that the thoughtform turns into a living entity with intelligence and knowledge. However, the content of the thought-form is a result of the projection and the impressing of the thoughtform with ideas, knowledge, and intelligence by the builder or builders. The result is that the thoughtform seems to have these qualities, where in reality it does not.

Any individual person, and more easily a group of people, can create a thoughtform that transmits certain ideas, visions, or direction. By remote control the thoughtform lives and moves and thinks, charged by the knowledge and visualization of its builder or builders.

Such a thoughtform is not dangerous in the beginning. But as it gradually relates with mediums and begins automatically to transmit its contents, it comes to the attention of dark forces. These dark forces see the best opportunity for themselves to create confusion, disturbances, and distortion in people who are being led by the *real* Leader, Master, or Initiate. As a result, the entire group, organization, or church is disintegrated by these messages through the mediums. The dark forces thus attract people with whatever good was contained in the thoughtforms and mix it with glamors, illusions, and contradictory statements. Many organizations devoted to such thoughtforms eventually disintegrate and perish. Only higher psychics can easily recognize such thoughtforms and either stay away from them or destroy them in Space, if they are trained to do so.

Masters, Initiates, Leaders, as well as some organizations, have their thoughtforms built by their devotees and their followers. Sometimes these thoughtforms become "places" that certain psychics go to receive instruction, advice, and courage. Unfortunately, the same thing happens: The dark forces penetrate into the "organization" and begin to teach the visitors confusing things. When the visitors' confusion is increased, they bring confusion back into the actual organization and slowly pollute it.

Some people may have hatred toward the organization. This hatred also adds certain elements to the thoughtforms which are then easily used by dark forces to attack the organization.

These mediums are very dangerous people. Through their blindness and ignorance, they can bring dark forces close to the daily activities of people and cause great damage. These dangers can be avoided if there are people who are clairvoyant and clairaudient in the astral and mental planes and, discovering the nature of the thoughtform and the corpses, they warn those who may believe them.

Many ancient races have perished due to the contact of mediums with thoughtforms and shells.[1]

Some mediums are possessed by entities; others by the thoughtforms. Some clairvoyants see this. The thoughtform may disintegrate in their mental aura, but the entity will increase in power and slowly darken the entire aura.

Great Teachers give the following advice regarding psychism:

1. Do not force yourself to be a psychic until your powers flourish naturally.

2. Never manipulate your centers and never concentrate upon them.

3. Find a wise Teacher when you feel that you are ready for instruction.

4. Never use your powers to satisfy the curious or selfish interests of others.

5. Study the *Upanishads, The Bhagavad Gita, The New Testament,* the works of H.P. Blavatsky, Alice A. Bailey, Helena Roerich, and other such literature.

6. Learn how to meditate.

---

1. For more information, read *The Externalization of the Hierarchy,* by Alice A. Bailey (New York: Lucis Publishing Company, 1957), pp. 10-15.

7. Observe your moral life and do not be trapped in sex, vanity, greed, hatred, and fear. Such elements destroy the communication line between you and your Solar Angel.

8. Try to live in the light of your Solar Angel.

9. Do not talk about your own spiritual striving and discoveries with average people.

10. Any psychic experience must be reported to your Teacher and no one else.

11. Any psychic order revealed from the subjective realms must not be obeyed until your Teacher's advice is sought.

These eleven factors will protect you for a long time on your path.

A question may be asked: If the entity in the astral or mental body has left and the corpse has disintegrated and vanished, is it still possible to know about that entity?

The answer is yes, if one records "the imagination of the astral plane." This seems like a very strange expression, but it is true. The astral plane is impressed by the Akashic Records. This impression creates in the astral plane an associative linkage which we call "the imagination of the astral plane." If the medium tunes in to such an impression, he can collect quite a bit of information about that entity, thinking that he is in contact with the entity itself.

How can we know the difference?

Akashic Records are reflected in the stormy sea of the astral plane. Although they are genuine impressions, as soon as they touch the astral plane, they are distorted. In addition, the magnetic power of the astral plane adds many other impressions to the original impression through the Law of Association. Now we have reality mixed with imagination or other impressions which appears to be a logical story.

Those who are active in the astral plane can have great fun watching the comedy going on in the consciousness of the medium. Some workers in the astral plane study all such possibilities and closely watch the power of imagination to learn how nature functions and why.

It is even possible for some mediums to key into such imaginations and be trapped in automatic writing. The danger is that unstable, ever changing, and ever moving impressions eventually make the brain of the medium confused and disturbed. There is almost no cure for such conditions because the astral impressions, if once keyed into, keep the brain of the medium in constant confusion.

Mediums also contact the phantoms in the astral plane. These phantoms are created in the magnetism of the astral plane when people preserve corpses in mausoleums. The majority of such phantoms visit people and haunt them. We are told that most of the nightmares and hallucinations are caused by these phantoms.

Every object in the world has its astral correspondences. A corpse has its astral correspondence which is the phantom. It is very important that corpses on the physical plane be cremated. Similarly, corpses on the astral and mental planes must be burned away. It is only fire that purifies Space and minimizes the pollution produced by those who follow the path of vice, ego, vanity, separatism, and treason.

To clarify further the conditions existing after death as well as the problems of mediums, let us deal with the soul when he leaves his body.

There are three periods in the interval between death and rebirth:

1. The human soul entering the astral plane.

2. The gestation period.

3. The state of *devachan*, when the higher nature of man enters a higher sphere to pass time in joy and bliss. Here it is that his worldly past fades away.

The gestation period is the period between the end of the astral plane and the beginning of *devachan*. Actually, the gestation period is in the lower mental plane, and a soul's duration there depends on the stored motives by which he did things while on earth. By what motive was help or money given to someone? What was the motive behind the gossip and slander? If the motives were selfish, harmful, and separative, the human soul stays a long time in the lower mental plane. If the motives were pure, the human soul enters into the *devachan,* which is the higher mental plane, the paradise, or the place where angels dwell.

So the gestation period is a preparatory period in which man clearly sees what his motives were in doing, saying, and thinking things in his life on earth. The important point is that this period is *controlled* by what a man did or did not do in his earth life and with what motive.

At the end of the gestation period the lower mental body is discarded. This is another death, the death of all that is not in harmony with the higher laws and principles.

There is a point here to be considered. If the Antahkarana has been built between the mental unit in the lower mind and the mental permanent atom in the higher mind, the human soul does not "die" but consciously enters into *devachan* after a sudden explosion of his mental body, and in *devachan*, or after a new incarnation, he maintains his continuity of consciousness as if all states were a chain of one life. But if he had not built the Antahkarana, he experiences another death when his lower mental body separates from the higher mental body.

In *devachanic* life, the human soul can have glimpses of the glory that *he is—in the future.* A contact is made with his Core, and the future vision of what he can be flashes into his consciousness.

Now coming back to mediums, some mediums can enter into the astral plane and communicate with the dead. But an Arhat, if for any reason He wants to, can enter into the *gestation* period and communicate with the soul of the departed one. The *devachanic* state is never disturbed. Generally, all that a medium materializes is one of the dead bodies of the disembodied human soul. In case of trance mediums, it is a floating corpse in the subtle worlds that is contacted.

Mediums can communicate with the dead only during the period between death and the astral existence, and from the astral existence to the door of the *gestation* period, when the soul is in the lower mental realms. The biggest probability is that the medium communicates with shells or corpses.

If the medium is really pure, he may contact the human soul when the soul is still in the astral or mental plane, but if there is impurity in him, he attracts the corpse to himself.

If the medium is pure, the disembodied soul may give messages to the soul of the medium and the medium uses his hands automatically to write down the messages given. Thus his hands are controlled while he is in higher spheres. The corpse also can occupy the medium's body and write messages through his hands. In both cases we are referring to messages that are given *not* by those who dwell in light, but average human beings whose horizon of consciousness is limited to the astral and mental planes. The danger is that in using the image of the known dead person, some dark forces can come in contact with the medium, and occupy and possess his body. Astral and mental corpses may do the same and eventually make the life of the medium miserable.

9

Automatic Writing

Most of the automatic writing is caused by the astral shell of a disembodied human being. Mediums attract such shells who control their hands and give messages according to the degree of development of the soul who left the shell. The majority of these messages have no value and if continued for a few years, one can see how confused the messages become.

It is also possible that a very advanced living person, with the permission of the *medium,* can occupy the medium's body and use his hand for certain messages, if the medium is not clairaudient or clairvoyant or if the message requires, because of its nature, writing through the medium's hand. Such messages are highly advanced. They have integrity, continuity, pure logic, and deep information about the particular subject. These are very rare cases. They happen when there is a dire need for guidance, and there is a unique medium whose body is pure enough to bear the high tension resulting from being occupied by an advanced soul.

Most of the automatic writings are useless or even less than mediocre. Sometimes the medium can write better things than his "guide" or "spirit." But often mediums are so enslaved with the obsessing "spirit" that they cannot see the mediocrity and the nonsense of the message. Instead of automatic writing, people must go deep into their own inner divinity. In every human being there are treasures which must be brought out into expression.

Some mediums wonder how a *shell* can know a person's secrets. Suppose the medium has a customer and he wants to test the "spirit" by asking it the customer's father's name. The spirit correctly tells him his father's name and is admired for the "knowledge." For esotericists this is a very simple matter. Because the customer knows his own father's name, he impresses the shell and the shell reflects the name into the brain of the medium and the medium transmits it to his customer.

What is an astral corpse which is sometimes called an astral shell? An astral corpse is a living elemental which is in the process of disintegration. This process takes time. The more earthly elements the corpse has, the longer it lives. Earthly elements are hate, fear, anger, jealousy, revenge, greed, malice, etc. These are elements which keep it alive or nourished and make it attractive to the sphere of earth. The purer the astral body, the shorter it lives. An astral body may explode and vanish in a second when the soul leaves it on the astral plane.

This semi-living entity operates fully when in the vicinity of human beings, affecting their astral body and trying to control it. Some of them are even absorbed in the astral body of a human being, causing violent and abnormal emotions in the person.

The astral corpse has its own centers and senses which are not fully developed but are developed enough to activate astral centers and senses in the human astral body. The astral corpse is a very sensitive instrument which may still tape events and play them back through the living human mechanism.

Scientists will eventually discover that the astral corpse plays a big role in human diseases. Astral corpses carry many astral germs, viruses, and even microbes which they transmit to those with whom they come in contact. Such germs, viruses, and microbes attach themselves to astral bodies and eventually manifest in the physical body.

It is interesting to know also that when a corpse attracts to itself the ectoplasm of the medium in a seance room, the appearing corpse is often seen in the same clothing which its body used to wear when alive.

The reason for this is that when people pass away and realize they are living, they imagine themselves wearing certain clothes of their choice. Such an imagination provides them with the clothes, and in the astral plane they appear with these clothes. When the soul loses the astral body, the astral body may still wear the same clothes. A medium, if he or she deals with such an astral corpse, will notice over time that it does not change its clothes, and the clothes become slowly more pale.

It is the entity in the astral body that imagines and through imagination creates any form he wishes to have, and when he leaves the astral body, it does not have the same capacity to create things.

Real communication is received when a person begins to operate on the abstract levels of mind. Here his message is telepathic, and first he contacts his Soul and then through his Soul he contacts his Master or advanced Initiates.

Here, as well as in the astral plane, it is easy to receive messages from disincarnate entities. Most of the trance mediums are in contact with those astral entities who did not yet leave their astral bodies. Some trance mediums, those who are not on abstract mental planes and are not in contact with their Souls, can contact disincarnate human beings in the lower mental plane. In both cases, their messages are very common and nothing new or higher comes from them. We must remember that in these two cases it is not the disincarnated human soul who is coming in contact with the medium on the physical plane, but it is the medium who is penetrating into the astral or lower mental plane and contacting disembodied souls. These disincarnated souls, if they are lingering on such planes, are generally average souls, and one cannot learn much from them.

The need at the present is for those advanced human beings who can go beyond the mental plane and contact those elevated beings who are ready to help humanity in any way possible. Such are people who worked very hard in the past and, with their conscientious and regular meditation and dedicated service, built their communication lines with the Higher Worlds and enabled themselves to withdraw from lower levels and consciously work on higher planes.

Beyond the mental plane, we find Those Who have finished Their human evolution and now work for Their planetary and solar education and train for service. We find also angelic beings whose contact with us transforms our life and fills our heart with the Divine Fire of Enthusiasm. The real training of the human souls starts after they graduate from the mental plane. This is why we are told that every aspirant for the greater vision must cultivate his mind, the lower and higher, trying to illuminate it with the light of Intuition.

10

Psychic Powers

No one can claim that he is a true psychic unless he uses all his powers and abilities for the service of humanity and for the fulfillment of the Hierarchical Plan.

All psychic powers that some individuals have cultivated by mechanical ways and means will increase the suffering and pain on earth, if the foundation of their power is not the unfoldment of the Divine Presence in them. This unfoldment expresses itself as pure intelligence and an all embracing love and the power to keep the personality in line with the spiritual goals.

There are many attempts to control the minds of other people through psychic powers. There are attempts to use psychic powers for political ends. All these will lead humanity toward global destruction if the true psychics do not appear and show us the purpose of life, and the ways and means that the purpose can be worked out.

Higher psychism can never be achieved if the tendency to violate the freedom or the wills of others exists in one's heart.

Before true psychism can flourish, man must demonstrate deep tolerance, inclusive love, a long life of sacrifice and renunciation, and a will that no glamor, illusion, or any hindrance can overcome.

It is very interesting to know that higher psychic powers are concealed in higher mysteries. They cannot be *taken* by our endeavors, or efforts, but they can be *given* to us if we are able to stand at the portals and knock on the doors. Those who give us the higher powers at the time of our initiation into higher mysteries meet in council, check our past records, see our future, and only then, if agreed, bestow higher powers upon us. To have higher powers means to be connected with higher centers of energy.

This is exactly the opposite of the cravings of those who sit and wait for psychic development and prepare many future incarnations for themselves full of pain, suffering, and frustration.

In the real spiritual evolution, you cannot enter into the higher mysteries until you are considered worthy by the Spiritual Hierarchy of the planet, the Head of which is the Christ.

This does not mean that we will wait and not strive. It means just the opposite. We must purify our physical, emotional and mental life, engage ourselves in sacrificial service, prove to ourselves that we are deeply interested in the welfare of one humanity, live a creative life, and expand our consciousness through meditation and service—and soon we will find ourselves led to the door of the Mysteries. At that stage the electrical network has been organized in us. They will turn the switches on if we are worthy to pass through the gate. It is very interesting to know that at the gate we will be enlightened to such a degree that we will see for ourselves if we are worthy to enter.

The attainment of true psychic powers is not like going to the bazaar and buying the things you want.

As humanity proves itself safe, more and more mysteries will be opened for entrance.

In the light of these ideas, how futile are the efforts of those who try to cultivate certain powers through breathing exercises, or through various yogas and disciplines.

No true power can be achieved unless the divinity in you is in steady expression. We become divine by *expressing* divinity in our life.

One may ask, "How did the followers of the left hand path, such as the Black Magicians, develop psychic powers?" The answer is that the Black Lodge, seeing that some people cultivated enough indifference to the sufferings of humanity, bestowed on them the astral and mental equivalents of machine guns, poison gases, chemical weapons, atomic bombs, powers that can violate privacy, insecticides, pesticides, and other such powers and taught them how to use these.

The point I want to stress is that the powers of the Black Magicians are not the result of their unfoldment. But the power of the White Magician is the extension of his True Self. The White Magician wins. The White Magician *earns* his powers. The Black Magician receives them. The White Magician does the work with his own powers. The Black Magician works with the power of the Black Lodge and its servants. That is why, when the Black Lodge takes away the power from a Black Magician, he becomes an ordinary man, but when a White Magician develops his powers, no power can take them away. His powers are the parts of the Self.

A White Magician is a highly developed person who uses his powers, his knowledge, and the laws of nature to lead humanity—

from darkness to light

from the unreal to the real

from death to immortality

from chaos to beauty

A White Magician is a graduated higher psychic.

Psychic power requires psychic energy. One must develop psychic energy if he wants to be a real White Magician—through meditation, sacrificial service, and studying the *book of life* and the laws that manifest therein.

We are told that one of the corrupting agents of psychic energy is inaction, laziness. When we withdraw into inaction and laziness, psychic energy dissipates and leaves our physical and emotional mechanisms in fatigue, in an exhausted state. People think that rest is inaction and laziness, but the real meaning of rest is equilibrium. In rest you use a different muscle of your body, a different vehicle of your constitution to balance your mechanism and charge the parts that need energy. Whenever the mechanism is balanced, psychic energy regenerates the whole system.

One of the secrets of health is to know how to turn on various parts of the whole mechanism rhythmically.

Psychic energy passes from one person to another through their handshake and other contacts, even through eye contact.

Psychic energy condenses in our nerve channels and emanates through our palms and fingers. People can heal others, if they have enough psychic energy, not only through their hands but also through their eyes.

All true psychic powers are the fruits of psychic energy.

Without psychic energy one can perform "miracles" but not the miracle of enlightening, transforming others, and revealing in them the sleeping Divine Presence.

— 11 —

Contact with Higher Worlds

Often we need to contact Higher Worlds to contact higher energies for our creativity. The best methods available for us are the following:

1. To expand our consciousness

2. To practice occult meditation

3. To exercise compassion, mercy, affinity, and love

4. To enter into the state of admiration

5. To increase joy and labor

6. To try always to live and think in beauty and freedom

7. To practice inclusiveness

These are the seven steps through which one is led to the gates of the Higher Worlds. Each of them singly as well as collectively can put a person in contact with energies that bring transformation and transfiguration on earth. Each of them brings into manifestation the spirit of cooperation and synthesis.

One does not need to communicate with disembodied spirits or with astral entities to find direction or protection. They all belong to the lower strata of consciousness.

Real guidance comes through these seven steps when they are practiced and continuously meditated upon. Each step releases an essence from our subtle vehicles which serves as an element of contact with Higher Worlds.

Higher Worlds have a different form of communication, such as through

1. Illumination

2. Bliss

3. Precipitation of Ideas

4. Energy

5. Joy

6. Impression

7. Inspiration

Contact with the Higher Worlds offers freedom. No formulated thoughts, words, and sentences are imposed upon you. It is you, according to your own karma and expansion of consciousness, who will use these seven blessings and formulate your treasury of wisdom.

The Higher Worlds extend like an ocean of blessings in front of you. You can use these blessings according to the need of the time. If you cultivate the power to make your contact steady with the Higher Worlds, you will never trap yourself by formulating these blessings into dogma and doctrines, but you will formulate these blessings into beauty, joy, freedom, light, courage, daring, wisdom, cooperation, vision, and organized labor.

The *partial contact* with the wisdom of those who are in steady contact with Higher Worlds is responsible for all the literature and activities which are built upon the foundation of self-interest, glamor, and illusion. Contact with Higher Worlds builds in us directness, purity of thought, clear vision, selflessness, harmlessness, simplicity, and humility.

These qualities do not let us present ourselves as more than what we are in consciousness and beingness. Therefore all that we do falls in with the Plan and is dedicated to One Humanity.

ABOUT THE AUTHOR

This is Torkom Saraydarian's latest published book. Many more will be released very soon. His vocal and instrumental compositions number in the hundreds and are being released.

The author's books have been used all over the world as sources of guidance and inspiration for true New Age living based on the teachings of the Ageless Wisdom. Some of the books have been translated into other languages, including German, Dutch, Danish, Portuguese, French, Spanish, Italian, Greek, Yugoslavian, and Swedish. He holds lectures and seminars in the United States as well as in other parts of the world.

Torkom Saraydarian's entire life has been a zealous effort to help people live healthy, joyous, and successful lives. He has spread this message of love and true vision tirelessly throughout his life.

From early boyhood the author learned first-hand from teachers of the Ageless Wisdom. He has studied widely in world religions and philosophies. He is in addition an accomplished pianist, violinist, and cellist and plays many other instruments as well. His books, lectures, seminars, and music are inspiring and offer a true insight into the beauty of the Ageless Wisdom.

Torkom Saraydarian's books and music speak to the hearts and minds of a humanity eager for positive change. His books, covering a large spectrum of human existence, are written in straightforward, unpretentious, clear, and often humorous fashion. His works draw on personal experiences, varied and rich. He offers insight and explanations to anyone interested in applying spiritual guidelines to everyday life. His no-nonsense approach is practical, simple, and readily accessible to anyone who is interested in finding real meaning in life.

Torkom Saraydarian has de-mystified the mysteries of the Ageless Wisdom. He has made the much needed link between the spiritual and the everyday worlds.

Look for exciting new books and music being released by Torkom Saraydarian.

GLOSSARY

Ageless Wisdom: The sum total of the Teachings given by great Spiritual Teachers throughout time. Also referred to as the Ancient Wisdom, the Teaching, the Ancient Teaching.

Akashic Records: Existing in the Higher Cosmic Ethers, the Akashic Records are living records of all experiences and activities that have ocurred in the past, present, and future of this planet and everything in it.

All-Self: See Cosmic Self.

Angelic Kingdom: Refers to beings following a different line of evolution than the human family.

Antahkarana: The path, or bridge, between the higher and lower mind, serving as a medium of communication between the two. It is built by the aspirant himself. It is threefold: the consciousness thread, anchored in the brain; the life thread, anchored in the heart; and the creative thread anchored in the throat. More commonly called the Rainbow Bridge.

Arhats: Ancient term designating Fourth Degree Initiates.

Aryan: Refers to the present period of the development of the human race. The Ageless Wisdom divides human development into seven sections, called Root Races. From ancient times to the present, they have been called: Polarian Race, Hyperborian Race, Lemurian Race, Atlantean Race, Aryan Race, Sixth Root Race, and Seventh Root Race. The latter two are the future states of human development. (For more information, see *Psyche and Psychism* by Torkom Saraydarian.)

Ashram: Sanskrit word. Refers to the gathering of disciples and aspirants which the Master collects for instruction. There are seven major Ashrams, each corresponding to one of the Rays, each forming groups or foci of energy.

Astral body: The vehicle composed of astral substance, that in which the emotional aspect of humanity expresses itself. Also known as the subtle body and the emotional body.

Astral Plane: The sixth plane of the Cosmic Physical Plane, in which the emotional processes are carried on. Sometimes called the astral or emotional world. Also known as the Subtle World or the Astral Realm or the Emotional Realm.

Atlantis: (Atlantean Epoch). The continent that was submerged in the Atlantic ocean, according to the occult teaching and Plato. Atlantis was the home of the Fourth Root Race, whom we now call the Atlanteans.

Aura: The sum-total of all emanations from all the vehicles of any living thing.

Black Lodge: See Dark Forces.

Chakra: Energy vortex found in each vehicle, relating to a particular part of the human body. There are seven primary chakras starting from the top of the head: (1) crown, (2) brow, (3) throat, (4) heart, (5) navel, (6) generative organs, (7) base of spine.

Chalice: See Lotus.

Clairaudience: The ability to hear beyond the audible range of vibrations, and also the power to hear astrally, mentally, and intuitively.

Clairvoyance: The ability to see beyond the visible range of vibrations, and also the power to see astrally, mentally, and intuitively.

Core: The essence or spark of God within each being; the Monad.

Cosmic Ethers: The highest four levels of the human constitution are called (from 4 to 1) the Intuitional Plane (Fourth Cosmic Ether), the Atmic Plane (Third Cosmic Ether), the Monadic Plane (Second Cosmic Ether), and the Divine Plane (First Cosmic Ether).

Cosmic Heart: See Cosmic Magnet.

Cosmic Magnet: The invisible center of the Universe.

Cosmic Physical Plane: Refers to the totality of the seven subplanes of manifestation, from highest to lowest: Divine, Monadic, Atmic, Intuitive or Buddhic, Mental, Emotional or Astral, and Physical. Each with seven subdivisions, totaling 49 planes of manifestation.

Cosmic Self: That great Entity which pervades and sustains all things on all levels of existence.

Dark Forces: Conscious agents of evil or materialism operating through the elements of disunity, hate, and separativeness.

Deva: See Angelic Kingdom.

Disciple: A person who tries to discipline and master his threefold personality, and manifests efficiency in the field where he works and serves.

Divine Plan: See Plan.

Divine Self: See Monad.

Ectoplasm: The combined emanations of the lymph glands and the human aura. It functions as the communication line between the physical body and the subtle body.

Ego: The human soul identified with the lower vehicles (physical, emotional, and mental) and their false values.

Emotional Body: See also Emotional Plane.

Etheric Body: The counterpart of the dense physical body, pervading and sustaining it. Formed by matter of the four etheric subplanes. The blueprint on which the physical body is based.

Fiery World: Refers to the Mental Plane or above. See Higher Worlds.

Great Ones: Beings who have taken the Fifth Initiation or beyond.

Guardian Angel: See Solar Angel.

Hierarchy: The spiritual Hierarchy, whose members have triumphed over matter and have complete control of the personality, or lower self. Its members are known as Masters of Wisdom Who are custodians of the Plan for humanity and all kingdoms evolving within the sphere of Earth. It is the Hierarchy that translates the Purpose of the Planetary Logos into a Plan for all kingdoms of the planet.

Higher Centers: Refers to the crown, brow, throat, and heart centers or chakras, as well as to the centers in the higher bodies.

Higher Realms: See Higher Worlds.

Higher Self: Refers to the Solar Angel or Transpersonal Self. See also Self.

Higher Spheres: See Higher Worlds.

Higher Worlds: Those planes of existence that are of a finer vibration of matter than the physical plane. Generally refers to the higher mental plane and above.

Human soul: See soul.

Initiate: A person who has taken an initiation. See also Initiation.

Initiation: The result of the steady progress of a person toward his life's goals, achieved through service and sacrifice, and manifested as an expansion of one's consciousness. It represents a point of achievement marked by a level of enlightenment and awareness. There are a total of nine Initiations that the developing human soul must experience in order to reach the Cosmic Heart.

Inner Core: See Core.

Inner Guide: See Soul.

Inner Presence: The Solar Angel. See Soul.

Karma, Law of: The Law of Cause and Effect or attraction and repulsion. "As you sow, so shall you reap."

Lemurian Epoch: A modern term first used by some naturalists and now adopted by Theosophists to indicate an era dealing with the period of the continent Lemuria, which preceded Atlantis. The Third Root Race.

Logos, Solar: The Core of the whole Solar System and all that exists in the Solar System. His purpose is to integrate, correlate and synchronize all Centers using His Light, Love, Power—like an electrical energy—to circulate within each atom through all Centers, thus revealing the Purpose for existence and challenging all forms to strive toward the highest form of cooperation.

Logos, Planetary: The Soul of the planet. The planet is His dense physical body to provide nourishment for all living forms.

Lotus: Also known as the Chalice. Found in the second and third mental plane (from the top). Formed by twelve different petals of energy: three love petals, three knowledge petals, three sacrifice petals. The innermost three petals remain folded for ages. They are the dynamic sources of these outer petals. The Lotus contains the essence of all of a person's achievements, true knowledge, and service. It is the dwelling place of the Solar Angel.

Lower Psychism: The ability to perceive subtle aspects of existence with the aid of the lower centers in the human body. Mediums, channels, etc. are considered lower psychics.

Lower self: The personality vehicles of the human soul. See also the self.

Masters: Individuals Who had the privilege to master their physical, emotional, mental, and Intuitional bodies.

Maya: A counterpart of illusions and glamors on the etheric plane. It results in the inability of the physical, emotional, and mental bodies to respond clearly to incoming impressions.

Meditation: Technique to penetrate the mind of the planet and develop creative abilities to manifest that mind in the life of humanity. (For in-depth information, please refer to *The Science of Meditation* and *Psyche and Psychism* by Torkom Saraydarian.)

Mediumistic: A tendency of certain individuals to astral phenomena and its perception thereof. Mediumistic people can, without guidance, fall into various dangers and traps associated with the astral plane. (For more information, see *Psyche and Psychism* by Torkom Saraydarian.)

Mental Body: The vehicle composed of the substance of the mental plane in which humanity expresses itself through thought.

Mental Plane: There are seven planes through which a human being travels and which make up human consciousness. From the lowest level upward, they are called: Physical, Emotional or Astral, Mental, Intuitional or Buddhic, Atmic, Monadic, Divine. The Mental Plane itself is divided into seven levels. The first three from the bottom are numbers seven, six, and five, which form the Lower Mental Plane. Number four is the middle mind or link. Numbers three, two, and one form the Higher Mental Plane.

Mental Realms: See Mental Plane. Also known as the Fiery World.

Mental Unit: A mental mechanism in the 4th level of the mental plane which is formed of four kinds of forces, and relates man to the sources of these four forces through its four spirillae.

Mind, Higher and Lower: See Mental Plane.

Monad: See Self.

Nirvana: The plane of consciousness known as the Atmic Plane.

Occultism: Term used to designate the Ageless Wisdom and its study. See Ageless Wisdom.

One Self: The universal Life Soul pervading all existence.

Permanent Atoms: Each body of a human being has one permanent atom which is the archetype for the construction and constitution of that vehicle.

Personality: Totality of physical, emotional, and mental bodies of man.

Petals: See Lotus.

Plan: The formulation of the Purpose of the Planetary Logos into a workable program—a Plan—by the Planetary Hierarchy for all kingdoms of nature.

Planetary Soul: See Logos, Planetary.

Purpose: That which the Solar Logos is intended to achieve at the end of the evolution of the Solar System. The Plan is the formulation of this Purpose for our planet only.

Race: The Ageless Wisdom divides human development into seven sections, called Root Races. From ancient times to the present, they have been called: Polarian Race, Hyperborean Race, Lemurian Race, Atlantean Race, Aryan Race, Sixth Root Race, Seventh Root Race. The latter two are the future states of human development. (For more information, see *Psyche and Psychism* by Torkom Saraydarian.)

self: The small "s" self is the sumtotal of the physical, emotional, and mental bodies of man. Commonly called the "lower self" or personality.

Self: The capital "S" Self is another term used to refer to the Core of the human being. The true Self is the developing, unfolding human soul who is trying to liberate himself, go back to his Father, and become his true Self.

Seven Fields of Human Endeavor: The expression of the Seven Rays in human evolution, each corresponding to a specific Ray. They are: Politics, Education and Psychology, Philosophy, Arts, Science, Religion, Economics and Finance.

Seven Rays: These are the seven primary Rays through which everything exists. They are pure energy, vibrating to a specific frequency and condensing from plane to plane, from manifestation to manifestation. The three primary Rays or Rays of Aspect are: The First Ray of Power, Will and Purpose; The Second Ray of Love-Wisdom; The Third Ray of Active, Creative Intelligence. There are four Rays of Attribute: The Fourth Ray of Harmony through Conflict; The Fifth Ray of Concrete Science or Knowledge; The Sixth Ray of Idealism or Devotion; The Seventh Ray of Synthesis or Ceremonial Order. These Rays indicate qualities that pertain to the seven fields of human endeavor or expression.

Shamballa: Known as the White Island, it exists in etheric matter and is located in the Gobi desert. Shamballa is the dwelling place of the Lord of the World, Sanat Kumara, and is the place where "the Will of God is known."

Solar Angels: Very advanced beings who sacrificed their life, descending from Higher Worlds to help the evolution of humanity, and guide its steps toward initiation. This happened on our planet at the middle of the Lemurian period. They are also called Guardian Angels, or Flames.

soul: The small "s" soul is the human psyche, the Spark, traveling on the path of evolution having three powers: will-power, attraction, and intelligence to guide its development. Also known as the evolving human soul.

Soul: Also known as the Solar Angel.

Soul Awareness: The human soul's awareness of the Solar Angel or the awareness of the human soul in the Intuitional Plane.

Spark: Human Monad fallen into matter.

Spiritual Triad: The field of awareness of the human soul. This field comes into being when the magnetic fields of the Mental Permanent Atom, the Buddhic Permanent Atom, and the Atmic Permanent Atom fuse and blend.

Subtle World: Refers to the Astral or Emotional plane.

Three-fold personality: The three vehicles of man. The combined forces and vehicles in which the evolving human soul expresses himself and gains experience during incarnation. These vehicles are the physical body, the emotional or astral body, and the mental body.

Transpersonal Self: The Solar Angel, the Inner Guide.

Treasure House: Symbolic term for the Chalice. Also called the Treasury.

Upanishads: Mystical treatises forming the *Veda*, said to date approximately from the Sixth Century, B.C. *The Upanishads* are said to be the source of all six systems of Hindu philosophy.

Vedas: Consists of four collections of writings: the *Rig-Veda,* the *Sama-Veda,* the *Yajur-Veda,* and the *Athar-Vaveda. The Vedas* are the Divine Revelation of the scriptures of the Hindus, from the root *viv,* "to know," or "divine knowledge."

Index

A

O

Obsession - 54
Obstacles
   and ugly deeds - 27
Officers - 70
Omnipotence - 7, - 64
   and Self - 68
Omnipotent - 24
Omnipresence - 7, - 64
   expansion of - 67 - 68
Omnipresent - 24
Omniscience - 7, - 64
   and True Self - 67
Omniscient - 24
The One Consciousness - 23
One Humanity - 111
One Self - 67, - 82
Orientation - 37
Ouspensky - 37

P

Pain - 54, - 104
Paradise - 95
The Path - 75, - 82, - 88
   and psychics - 44
Patience - 15, - 18, - 44
Peace - 10
People
   effects of service - 55
Perfection
   model of - 69
   path of - 70
Permanent Atom
   Mental - 96
Permanent atoms - 41
Perseverance - 15, - 18, - 44
Personality - 13, - 61, - 64
   and mediums - 86
   defined - 13
Phantoms - 94
Philosophy - 68
Physical
   illnesses - 10
Physical body - 74, - 87
   and joy - 31
   as device for soul - 41
Physical ego - 40
Physical plane - 36

The Plan - 14, - 54, - 56, - 103, - 111
Planetary soul - 44
Planets
   sacred - 79
Plato - 67
Political - 68
Possession - 54
   of mediums - 80
Potentials
   cultivation of - 55
   latent - 69
   manifestation - 45
Potentials, higher
   defined - 56
Power - 33, - 60
Powers
   and archetypes - 70
   of human soul - 61
   physical - 5
   seven in man - 70
Prayers - 88
The Presence - 16
   in actions - 31
Prestige - 30
Problems
   solving of - 6
Prosperity - 63
Protection - 109
   from attacks - 74
Psyche - 5
   powers of - 7
Psychic - 15, - 42, - 60
   advanced - 37
   and consciousness - 14
   and dark forces - 54
   high quality - 54
   low level - 54
   manifestations - 63
   orders - 93
Psychic development - 104
Psychic energy - 19, - 60, - 106
   and miracles - 107
   corruption of - 106
   development of - 106
   regeneration of bodies - 106
Psychic potentials - 54
Psychic power
   and love - 9
Psychic powers - 11, - 13
   and animals - 58

Q

Other Works by **Torkom Saraydarian**

The Ageless Wisdom
Bhagavad Gita
Challenge For Discipleship
Christ, The Avatar of Sacrificial Love
A Commentary on Psychic Energy
Cosmic Shocks
Cosmos in Man
A Daily Discipline of Worship
Dialogue With Christ
Fiery Carriage and Drugs
Five Great Mantrams of the New Age
Flame of Beauty, Culture, Love, Joy
Hiawatha and the Great Peace
Hidden Glory of the Inner Man
Hierarchy and the Plan
Irritation—The Destructive Fire
I Was
Joy and Healing
Legend of Shamballa
The Psyche and Psychism
The Psychology of Cooperation and Group Consciousness
Questioning Traveler and Karma
Science of Becoming Oneself
Science of Meditation
The Sense of Responsibility in Society
Sex, Family and the Woman in Society
Spiritual Regeneration
Spring of Prosperity
Symphony of the Zodiac
Synthesis
Talks on Agni
Torchbearers
Triangles of Fire
Unusual Court
Woman, Torch of the Future

Next Release: **Toward The Year 2000**